EUROPE
THE RADICAL CHALLENGE

EUROPE

THE RADICAL CHALLENGE

Hugh Thomas

Weidenfeld and Nicolson
5 Winsley Street London W1

ISBN NO 0 297 76510 8

Printed in Great Britain by
Willmer Brothers Limited, Birkenhead

Contents

ACKNOWLEDGEMENTS   VII
INTRODUCTION   1

PART I

1	*The Political Challenge*	5
2	*The Institutions*	16
3	*The European Parliament*	28
4	*The Challenge of the Institutions*	42
5	*The US, Britain and Europe*	47
6	*Britain, Europe and the World*	51
7	*Defence of a New Europe*	66
8	*Europe and the Third World*	77
9	*Europe, the UN and World Prospects*	84

PART II

1	*Change in Society*	87
2	*Social Security and Labour*	93

PART III

1	*The Economic Problem*	106
2	*Social Democracy and Economic Growth*	116
3	*An Economic Analysis*	121
4	*The Multinational Company*	129
5	*Technology*	133
6	*Monetary Union*	137
7	*A Europe of Regions*	141
8	*Monopolies*	149
9	*Transport and Energy*	152
10	*Taxation*	155
11	*Growth and Environment*	159
12	*Agriculture*	165
13	*Economic Planning in Europe*	176
14	*The Alternatives*	181

CONCLUSION   188
NOTES   201
INDEX   203

Acknowledgements

This book owes a great deal to my research assistant, Carl Wilms-Wright, Weidenfeld scholar at the Graduate School for Contemporary European Studies at the University of Reading. Many of the good ideas in this book are his. He guided me brilliantly over much tricky ground. I am also very grateful to several people who kindly made helpful comments about the draft of the book.

Ana Maria Burrows, Joy Thelwall and my wife typed the book in record time.

Hugh Thomas, London, 24 October 1972

Introduction

Over the next five years, we shall be entering what is, for most of us, a new world. By 1978, Britain will be a full member of the European Economic Community, following our formal entry on 1 January 1973, and the passage of the European Communities Bill in July 1972.

Does this mean an end to a 'thousand years of history', as Hugh Gaitskell thought would be the case in 1962, at the time of Harold Macmillan's application to join the Community? And does it mean subordination to a large and clumsy organization over which we shall have no effective, and no democratic, control? Michael Foot, Peter Shore, and others have given eloquent expression to this danger in the debates on the European Communities Bill during the summer of 1972, pointing to the pile of regulations and directives already issued by the Community which will, from now on, have the force of law in our country.

This book agrees that our entry into the Community does represent an end to Hugh Gaitskell's famous thousand years, but argues that this ending is a welcome one; and that the question whether those years could be prolonged is doubtful, if the implication is one of a splendid, or imperial, isolation. The book admits that there is a serious danger that the anxieties of Michael Foot and his colleagues on the left of the Labour party will turn out to be firmly based unless we make a resolute attempt to make democratic ('democratize') and make political ('politicize') the European Community in a way which the present French government, and probably the present British government, seem to oppose in the name of national interest.

I suggest too that there is now only one serious political

possibility ahead of us: namely, to achieve a federal and democratic united community of Europe, in which the needs of different regions and classes are creatively realized. Everything else which immediately appears to be of great political moment, such as education, housing, inflation, labour relations, the environment, pales in comparison with this long-term political design, since these other things will, in the end, be determined absolutely by what sort of Europe develops after our entry.

The book is subtitled 'the Radical Challenge'. Contrary to what has seemed to be the case when reading the speeches in the European Communities Bill debates, and other contributions to the so-called 'Great Debate', it is suggested that our commitment to the European idea can really make possible the substantial and radical changes in society which everyone knows are needed, but which have not been achieved within the narrow and stifling apparatus of the nation state. The possibilities for social democracy as it was defined in, for example, the Labour election manifestoes of 1964, 1966 and 1970, are considerable; but they are even greater for that sort of 'new politics' which would set greater emphasis on the quality of life, both in work and at home, more economical use of scarce resources, and greater and more real rights at a local level.

Our entry into Europe opens up many exciting possibilities, both for ourselves and for the continental European countries, with one main proviso: that the British become very quickly 'whole hog' Europeans, seeking to outflank the narrow nationalism both of the present government and of other forces of nostalgia, from the Left, and from a position which is usually described as a federal one, though this word, like others in political usage, is liable to misrepresentation.

I am writing this book from a position quite outside the day-to-day political struggle. I have thought it essential, however, to say what seems simple and obvious, but which has not been said, so far as I have been able to discover, by other people who have been more closely involved in the European arguments over the last ten years. Perhaps this is because 'Europeans' in this country have spent their energies trying to persuade the Right that membership of the European community is in their interest, and particularly their financial interest. It only became clear late in the day that the most vigorous defenders of the idea of national sovereignty would be found on the Left in British politics, rather than on the Right. Furthermore, the accident of Labour politics has meant that the Europeans on the Left in Britain have recently been rather silent, in the hope that they would maintain the unity of the Labour movement by this reticence. The 'New Left', which has had a more forward-looking attitude than the 'Old Left' on this particular subject, has little real political strength.

I have investigated the whole range of future possibilities in Europe, at first the political position, then the social one, and finally the economic, though I am, of course, aware that these compartments are falsely divided. The political matter is the essential one, of course, and I discuss that first, looking in particular at the existing institutions of Europe, and how they should be improved – not because the social and economic sides to the discussion are inferior in importance, but because they are subject to political decisions. But all the problems should be considered together. For example, one can scarcely discuss the politics of the environment, the preoccupation of the early 1970s, without a consideration of the economic cost involved and the social priority that it assumes. This is what has prompted me to attempt, in the space of a single and short study, a general inquiry into a series of problems, each one of which has preoccupied writers and students of politics for many years. When speaking of the future of a country, however, and even more of a continent, a large number of subjects press themselves forward at the same time; and how each single one of them is to be resolved, and in what order, affects the treatment of the next matter. I am an amateur student of every subject discussed in this book. My excuse for writing is not only that politicians often seem to be amateurs too, but that an expert on one side of the problem, such as the European trade unions, would necessarily be an amateur on the others.

3

Since the book was finished, three events have occurred. The first was the Labour Party conference, at which the Party managed to avoid any explicit commitment to withdraw from the European Community when it returns to power. This skilful piece of tactics on the part of Mr Harold Wilson will not only save many Labour party members a great deal of embarrassment; it will make the return of the party to power much more likely. The second was the Paris summit, in October 1972, at which the governments of the Nine made very encouraging progress indeed towards the achievement of creative regional policies and monetary union; but made no progress at all on the political side of the question. The communiqué of the conference in a sense, therefore, gives the Labour movement, and all progressive parties in Europe, a new agenda for their own action: the outflanking of the existing governments in Europe, including our own, by pressing for the radical democratization of the community's institutions with the goal ahead of achieving not only a monetary union by 1980, but also a political community of a new kind to render that monetary union socially responsible.

The third occurrence is the beginning of serious speculation on the political needs of the new community in the British press and elsewhere. The publication in the *New Statesman* at the end of October 1972 of an article taken from *Agenor*, the vigorous left-wing monthly based in Brussels, certainly constitutes a milestone on the history of both those journals; it may do so within the history of the British Left, who may soon surely will begin to understand the undoubted fact that, while private enterprise has become international, radical politics remains obstinately national. The present book is a contribution to the discussion which will surely, and should surely, be a major preoccupation in this country and on the continent in the middle of the 1970s. It was written in the belief that the present structure of the nation state makes change for the better impossible in our acquisitive society; but that our full commitment to the creation of a new European community can be of the greatest benefit.

Part I

1 The Political Challenge

Britain refused to join the European Economic Community at its beginning in 1957, but has been trying to join it since 1961. She is also joining the Coal and Steel Community and Euratom. The first of these latter two organizations she also refused to join, at its inception in 1950 but became an 'associate'. She has been an associate of Euratom too, but has not taken it very seriously. In Britain's absence, the institutions of three undertakings joined in 1967, and further work has been done on the unmistakably political assumptions of these bodies' original founding treaties. However, as our good luck would have it, the political side of the new Europe has not been at all well developed, in contrast with its economic side. Perhaps good luck is the wrong word, since it was the same thing – the will power of de Gaulle reflecting a large section of French opinion – that kept Britain out of Europe for an extra ten years and also kept Europe from political growth. At all events, we are now able to be present at the next, if not the very earliest, stages of what happens.

The question is, upon the brink of what are we? A new unitary European state? A league of national states, determined to retain independence of each other in the last resort, linked only in a tariff-free customs union? A federal state, a federation of states, or a confederation? A community of some new kind? The truth is that all these things are possible within the next generation – even, perhaps, the first.

The case for political union needs examination. But it can be short. An economic policy, community or association is in-

5

conceivable without a political content. Economics without politics means either injustice or chaos, probably both. A tariff-free customs union is open to all sorts of political pressures, from within or without (by industry or banking or multinational companies), and would probably collapse. It could provide no security, nor permanent rights of access to the markets of the other nations concerned. Once the sky of world trade began to cloud over, tariffs would go up like umbrellas. A customs union would also mean shying away from a really exciting opportunity for political innovation, involving perhaps the rationalization of government expenditure, and of effort in advanced technology which, as Christopher Layton (now a member of Altiero Spinelli's cabinet in Brussels) has rightly argued, is one of the largest sources of waste in Europe: 'The international management of money and of companies will remain burdened by extra costs so long as taxes and laws are different and capital markets divided.' A free trade area, such as EFTA, allows complete freedom to states to make unilateral arrangements for duties on imports coming from outside the area.

It was obvious that, in power, the last Labour prime minister was aware of the implications of the economic union that he then favoured: 'Many of us feel,' he said, in a debate in the House of Commons in July 1969, 'that there is a case for developing institutions towards political unity in Europe.' He said much the same at a speech to the trade unions in January 1970: 'The country must develop in new fields, not only economic but political and defence too. . . . Our defence interests are identical, and our political interests are growing every day progressively closer. As we develop new policies together, we shall find it natural to develop the institutional machinery which we shall need to execute these policies – in the economic and monetary fields, in trade, in foreign policy and in defence.' The Labour party, therefore, in 1967 and in 1970, had, when in power, a more political and long-sighted attitude than the Conservative government had at the time of Macmillan's application to join the EEC in 1961–3 and in most ways more than Mr Heath has exhibited since 1970. Nor do I

6

believe that it was merely that, when in power, the Labour ministers simply read with docility the briefs prepared for them by Michael Palliser, Mr Wilson's principal foreign policy private secretary, and other officials of the time. Mr Wilson, in particular, and some other ministers sounded as if they really accepted that 'Britain should seek to play a leading part in building a Europe that would have the power to look after its citizens more effectively than individual nation states are now able to'.[1] Mr Wilson also took the critical decisions marking the virtual end of Britain's Far East role, and transferring the emphasis of Britain's defence interests to Europe.

The idea of a political union opens, to be practical, two possibilities: do we imagine a Europe united, as a federation, community or state, that is akin to existing nation states, such as the USA or the USSR? Or do we seek to establish, and keep, a 'Europe of States', a confederation, as President de Gaulle thought a maximum, and as President Pompidou also seems to regard as such, judging from recent though fairly casual, remarks? Or, hoping in the long run for the former, do we try and make do with the latter, for the forseeable future, hoping that it will do all we all want for our generation? Nevertheless, 'a map which does not contain Utopia has no validity', said Oscar Wilde, and, even if we wish to progress gradually, it is desirable to know where we are going. The *'Europe des états'* would be, perhaps is, a new type of political association, it is true, which might move, over the generations, towards a closer union. But it might not.

There are difficulties about both courses. A federated united states of Europe would be an unhappy creation, if it were simply to lead to a new, conventional nation state, comparable to the old nation states of the past, only bigger. The history of the nation state is on the whole unedifying, since it culminated in the two world wars which were, in a way that we have not yet fully appreciated, its logical conclusion. But a confederation might prevent, or delay, political will, as well as effective economic planning, not to speak of defence planning: further, by postponing democratic practices, in the name of national

7

interests, it would exacerbate the bureaucratic nature of the community, and give it less reality or legitimacy.

Federalism, it scarcely needs repetition, has had an old and radical past. Proudhon, whose phrase 'Property is Theft' made him one of the most famous fathers of socialism, argued that a federation of nations was essential in order, primarily, to guarantee the interests of smaller countries. Alliances, of the type which characterized the last years of the nineteenth century and the first of this, risked the subordination of small states to a great European monarchy. 'The twentieth century,' he wrote with much prescience, 'will open the era of federations, or mankind will once more begin a purgatory lasting a thousand years.'[2] Europe in fact avoided a 'thousand year purgatory' between 1933 and 1945 with some difficulty, and Britain, like France, has now emerged into the light of the second half of the century as a state whose freedom certainly has been limited by close attachment to the US.

Plans for international unity have indeed had a long history within the European Left. Trotsky hoped for a 'United Socialist States of Europe', and Aristide Briand proposed the idea, in general terms, in 1930. Before 1914, no articulate, and conscientious, reformer of any country would have failed to have included in his argument some variety of internationalism, some acceptance of the view that, in Anthony Crosland's words, socialism does not stop at the white cliffs of Dover. (Crosland's most important book, *The Future of Socialism*, did, however, stop just there.) These names, along with that of Proudhon, are widely enough spread to suggest that support of a wider, and international, grouping for our country is fully in the tradition of radical thought. The dream of a federal Europe after the war was also one of the inspirations of the European Resistance movements. Altiero Spinelli has recalled that, in the Resistance, even in Mussolini's prisons, he and his comrades were working for a 'free and united Europe'.[3] *Combat*, the French clandestine paper, made the same point. Europe may sometimes seem to have been rejuvenated by Conservatives or Catholics, such as Churchill, or Adenauer, or Schumann, but those active within

8

Nazi Europe before 1945 have an earlier claim. So too do those who fought against what they thought was the likely fascist domination of Europe in the International Brigades in Spain in the civil war.

In April 1972, Dr Mansholt, addressing the European parliament for the first time as President of the Commission, advocated the full removal of restrictions to travel within Europe's frontiers: 'Those who move from one country to another to work, must be able to exercise the ordinary rights of citizenship and should no longer be treated as foreign labour.' In this speech, he echoed exactly the call for travel free of passports made by Ernest Bevin when defining his aims as foreign secretary; Bevin, however, did nothing about the matter. The Community over which Dr Mansholt presided with such distinction has got closer to putting the idea into practice than anyone, even if it is only a first step towards a world-wide freedom which seems much more elusive.

The revival of the idea of federalism in the late 1940s was ineffective and, though some of its proponents spoke grandiosely, somewhat dull. The reason for the ineffectuality and the tedium is not far to seek: the federalists seemed mostly interested in a political and legal instrument, and not in the social or economic philosophy that, implicity or explicitly, lay behind it. The founders of the European movement in the 1940s – like most others – neglected regional questions, the problems of technology, environmental and health questions. Where they were adventurous, they were so only in the, in European circumstances then, somewhat unreal world of foreign policy: a Third Force sounded good, but in the late 1940s it could never have been a real strategy. Carried into practice, it might have been disastrous. The Europe which has, in the event, grown up on the inspiration of Jean Monnet's idea that the continent as a whole should profit from the great Rhine coal and iron fields, may be more materialistic than the federalists of the first generation after the war liked. But the material is often more substantial than the ideal.

There are, however, distinctions to be made among feder-

9

alists: on the one hand, democratic federalists, on the other, 'functionalists'. The latter are certainly interested in federalism, but their method of achieving it is based on what has been described as a functional approach to integration. They are less concerned with the self-assertion of democratic institutions, than with governmental contact and support. They are bureaucratic, technocratic, and preoccupied with élites. The Schuman plan, resulting in the Coal and Steel Community, was functionalist and, in many ways, the European Community as it now is itself has turned out functionalist, against the will of many of its founders and even operators. Its representatives, members of the Commission, may very well be sincere federalists, but their freedom of action is limited, and their progress slow.

Confederation, in its European sense, is an idea primarily associated with de Gaulle. But it is one typical of the conservative approach to Europe generally. The communiqués of M. Pompidou and Mr Heath seem to reflect desire for a confederation of states. Admittedly, we should not be too preoccupied by labels. Switzerland is a confederation, but its unity is stronger than that of some federations.

The leading proponents of the New Europe, however, are men whose 'ultimate purpose', in the words of the first president of the Commission of the Economic Community Walter Hallstein, 'is the creation of a European federal state'. Why? Because 'without such a state, it will be impossible to maintain lasting peace in, and for, Europe or to enable Europe effectively to maintain its position in the world'.[4] The word 'state' in this connection is, admittedly, unpromising, and it has had an evil history. The state is a cold monster. The word 'community' is, in fact, better: Europe should become a community with a will, a society with a capacity to decide, and with a collective direction, but a community of peoples, not of states.

It seems that, paradoxically, perhaps, Mr Heath, who has led Britain towards Europe, draws the line at federalism. 'Sir Alec in line with Pompidou,' ran a headline in the *Guardian* in 1972, alluding to a speech by the foreign secretary at the annual dinner of the Institute of Directors, at which he had implied that a 'firm decision' had been taken long ago in Downing Street that 'those who believe in European federalism with centralized parliamentary control will be beating their heads against a stone wall – at least while Mr Heath is in power'. But, in the same speech, Sir Alec, paradoxically enough, went on to boast how powerful the 'voice of Europe' could be on behalf of a community responsible for forty-one per cent of the world's trade. There is either an ambiguity here, or there is a clear statement that the future of Europe will be less than perfectly democratic. For if Europe evolves a will, or a voice even, its political system must be, to some extent, federal if it is to be democratic. Furthermore, the interest that the Conservative government has shown in the project for a European monetary union suggests that Mr Heath's apparent lack of interest in federalism may be only skin deep. Here, it seems, the government of Mr Heath may have a different outlook to that of Mr Macmillan, whose interests in a supranational Europe were, if anything, less than those of de Gaulle. (Sir Alec Douglas-Home, in this respect, has sounded more like Mr Macmillan than Mr Heath.)

The plunge towards what is usually known as federation may seem bound to be gradual while the Community relies on the member states and their traditional methods to put into effect their decisions. Does this mean that federal powers, including federal troops, are in the end essential? Or even in the beginning? There is an alternative: namely, a European currency controlled by the Community. To be realistic, too, it must be said that Europe will be preoccupied, for the next few years, with the already demanding task of integrating Britain and the other new members into the existing structure, taking into account the changes which will be demanded of the new members and the changes which will be caused in the 'Six'. There are also the consequences, many of them unfortunate, for other countries. The Community will take some time absorbing the new countries' quota of 'Eurocrats'.

The main argument against the political clauses, and the inevitable political implications, of the Treaty of Rome, is that they surrender British sovereignty and, in particular, the sovereignty of parliament. That is scarcely a socialist argument: 'No socialist will cling to national sovereignty for its own sake', remarked the Labour Party's NEC in 1962, and they were right. The argument about sovereignty is used by people on both sides of politics, extreme Left and extreme Right: it reminds one of the badly translated instructions in the lavatories of old French trains: 'To obtain water, turn indifferently to Left or Right'. It must be obvious that our signature of the Treaty of Rome does limit our national sovereignty. Those who argue that it does not have that effect, such as Sir Alec Douglas-Home, in a speech at Edinburgh in June 1972, or Lord Hailsham, in a speech to the Grotius dinner of the British Institute of International and Comparative Law, are deceiving themselves, or their hearers (Lord Hailsham's explanation, which could scarcely have seemed appropriate to that particular audience, was that the Community merely 'introduced a new source of law directly applicable in the municipal jurisdictions of the member states'). A treaty setting out to eliminate customs duties, to establish a common external tariff, and a common commercial policy, to abolish restrictions on the free movement of persons, capital services and so on, obviously constitutes a substantial sacrifice of sovereignty. Harold Wilson in 1967 pointed out to the House of Commons that our sovereignty has been affected by other things also: our alliances with France in the first part of the century, our membership of the League of Nations, of the UN, NATO, the OEEC, and other international organizations: while our decline, to become a power of the second, rather than of the first, rank, has limited that freedom of action which was a characteristic of Britain's international position in, say, 1890. Mr Wilson, in the debate in the House of Commons in August 1967, even commented lightly that the 'question is not whether sovereignty remains absolute or not, but in what way one is prepared to sacrifice sovereignty'. Today, even great powers, such as the US, have had their freedom of action limited by international agreements, and even by their commercial necessities. Freedom of action internationally has even sometimes seemed to be the prerogative of small states, like Israel or Cuba, rather than of the USA or of Russia, though perhaps that is mere appearance too. 'However garbled some of its explanations may be, it can hardly avoid being about fundamentals: it is about the nation and the state.' Thus Tom Nairn, in the *New Left Review* in 1971, in speaking of the debates about whether or not to join the Community. Further, though sovereignty may seem to us important, it does not look like that to many other states. Indeed, the world wars have depressed most continental Europeans about the notion of the sovereign nation state; and we have to thank not our sovereignty but the Channel, and Hitler's inability, or reluctance, to invade us before turning East, or our friendship with the US, that we did not enter the postwar era in that same mood. The great difference between Britain and continental Europe in 1945 was not that they had been under Nazi rule, while we had not: but that forward-looking people there realized that, in the words of Willy Brandt, 'the nation state was a thing of the past', while few of us saw that in Britain.[5] Altiero Spinelli has similarly pointed out that in the struggle of continental European democrats against totalitarianism 'the national loyalty of the anti-fascists' had been reduced to 'vanishing' point. Since fascism and Nazism had completely identified themselves with the state, to oppose these tyrannies meant necessarily to oppose the state itself.[6]

The consequence of the war was thus for even realists in all the European states, except Britain and Russia, to lose faith in the nation state as a viable political undertaking. The state had demanded everything from its citizens but had failed totally to preserve their liberty, their property and their lives, save by accident. Britain and Russia had very different experiences, and different starting points, Britain being democratic and capitalist, Russia being revolutionary and communist, but they did have in common a continuing tolerance of a political system which in many parts of Europe had been destroyed.

The consciousness of loss of British sovereignty has come much later. Mr Roy Jenkins, in his Henry L. Stimson lectures at Yale in 1971, recalled, however, how at meetings of the Group of

Nine, the principal rich monetary powers of the world, he was forced to wait, on occasion for hours, while the financial ministers of the Community made up their minds: 'I did not enjoy being shut out from a decision-making process which could be crucial to the future of Britain,' he said.[7] In this respect, therefore, British adherence to the Community is an attempt to recover mastery over her own fate. Mr Harold Wilson surely appreciates that too: in a speech in the Commons while still prime minister, he said that the whole history of political progress is a history of gradual abandonment of national sovereignty.

There are those who believe that Europe has no political stability, and that it would be fatal for proud, secure and happy Britain to join with her in any permanent association. This argument was put with a special vigour, and venom, by Clive Jenkins in a speech which he should be ashamed of having made, at the Brighton Trades Union Congress in 1970: 'We are being invited to join a France which has twice in a decade been brought to the brink of civil war, an Italy with a social structure now so obsolete as to be virtually ungovernable, a Holland with a parliament split into warring factions, a Belgium riven by a agony of politics, religion and language, and a Germany with an uneasy coalition between a Social Democratic party and a right-wing market force-articulated bourgeois party.' Clive Jenkins went on to make several contemptuous (and contemptible) comments on the then commissioners of the Community, which make clear that he knew nothing, and really cared nothing, about them.[8] That sort of language is irresponsible, nationalistic, and unworthy of anyone in a position of influence and power such as the general secretaryship of the Association of Scientific Technical and Managerial Staff must be supposed to have. A similar point of view was expressed by Paul Johnson in the course of a personal attack on Roy Jenkins in the *New Statesman* in May 1972.[9]

Comments of that sort are not only historically untrue but inappropriate in a generation which has seen the appearance of such Social Democrats as Willy Brandt, Sicco Mansholt,

Altiero Spinelli and others, all of whom are men of a moral stature at least as great as anyone produced by the British Labour party. Similarly, a case could be made that the men of the Commission are on average more enlightened than are most ordinary civil servants. A man such as Georges Berthoin, the permanent representative of the European Communities in London until 1973, can fairly claim to have transcended national interests.

2 The Institutions

The institutions of the European Community present a series of intricate puzzles. At present, the Commission in Brussels, composed of civil servants internationally recruited, makes proposals to a Council of Ministers composed of representatives of the national governments. The relation between Commission and Council of Ministers is an abnormal one for several reasons: first, the Commission prepares the agenda for, and puts up ideas to the Council, which can seldom act except on a proposal by the Commission; second, the Council is served by the committee of permanent representatives, really ambassadors, of the member countries to the Community, who have collectively made themselves into a major organ in the Community; and, third, the Commissioners, the directors of the work of the Commission, are mainly politicians rather than civil servants – men who have been bent on developing, or articulating, the power of the Community. The work of the Council is rendered more complicated by the principle of unanimous voting which has evolved since the crisis of 1965–6 in the Community. In practice, all proposals are discussed in the committee of permanent representatives of the member states until agreement is reached and then *pro forma* submitted to the members of the Commission. There is also the European Court of Justice, an Economic and Social Committee, many other committees and the European Parliament.

The inter-relation between these bodies is complex and rendered more so because the influence of one or other of them is directly related to the hopes or fears that are entertained for the future of the Community generally. Power to the Council of Ministers seems to betoken confederation, power to the Commission seems on the surface to suggest federation. The institutions are, as can be seen even from this brief description, fundamentally different from those of nation states, and that fact by itself makes it more likely that, through the EEC, we have a chance of improving on the nation state's shortcomings. These institutions are themselves, however, far from perfect, and their practice is in serious need of revision and improvement. But they are probably with us to stay. It is no use wishing now that European unity could be started anew, or built upon other foundations than these. Our freedom of action is thus already limited by several years of experience from which we, the British, chose to exclude ourselves in the beginning. At the same time, these existing institutions of the Community, as it now is, have attached to them the vigorous enthusiasm of almost a generation of enlightened men.

The Council of Ministers has had such power in the Community of Europe as has hitherto existed. It is already more than a mere governmental conference, since it has permanent status enshrined in a treaty. It has legislative characteristics, in the sense that it can adopt legislative proposals and make them binding, though it does this formally, in secret, as if it were a Cabinet not an assembly, with the 'leak' the only communication about the discussion. The combination of practices which has been introduced (some decisions to be unanimous, some to be by simple majority, some again by a qualified majority) has given the Council some flexibility, though majority voting has been used only rarely, and on very minor matters. In fact, decisions have been difficult to secure. For example, the Commission proposed a scheme for the revision of European agriculture in December 1968, in a plan entitled 'Agriculture 1980' (the Mansholt plan), but the first steps to put these proposals into effect were only taken in March 1972. Controversial decisions – whether or not to establish a regional aid fund, as insisted upon by the Italians, whether to have a political secretariat – have been continually postponed.

The Council has failed to reach a decision on some three hundred of the Commission's proposals, and has not even discussed well over a hundred of them.

The danger is that the Council of Ministers will remain the major centre of operations of the Community, and that governments will concentrate such inventive power as they have upon it rather than upon, say, the European parliament. Thus, with the air of making a revolutionary proposal, the Belgian government has recently suggested that the Presidency of the Council of Ministers should rotate at twelve-monthly intervals, instead of every six months for every member country, as at present. The Belgians believe that the President of the Council of Ministers elected for a year, should always be a senior cabinet minister designated by his country specially to preside there, rather than be, as at present, the foreign minister, who is obviously busy with a host of other things. This President of the Council, the Belgians think, should devote his time to co-ordinating the work of the Council. But that would, at best, simply make the Council stronger, but would not necessarily make for greater political integration.

There is also the idea, first suggested by M. Pompidou and then taken up by Herr Brandt, that governments should designate 'European Ministers', who, with Cabinet rank, should be permanently responsible for European matters. This idea is superficially attractive, but probably the influence of such ministers at home would be small. Within the Community, they would be presumably less influential than the foreign ministers, and, if they were not members of the Council, their appointment would merely lead to one more intermediate, intergovernmental body between the Council and the Commission. The proposal would indeed give to the process of integration an intergovernmental, rather than a really international, character.

Another, much more far-reaching, proposal is that the Council or at least the President of the Council should be nominated by the European parliament. The motive for the suggestion is, of course, that it would assist in the democratization of the Community. In practice, the idea would be unlikely to be accepted by the European governments for the forseeable future. The office of President is at the moment a temporary one, and so powerful ministers perhaps would be reluctant to take it on. The consequence might be to destroy such power as the Council now has.

As to what we should hope might be done to the Council of Ministers, we should distinguish between short-term improvements and long-term plans, the first, of course, to lead, if possible, to the latter. The Council should operate with representatives of the European parliament present, as well as members of the Commission, as at the moment. Its proceedings should as a rule be published verbatim. The present system of leaks is ridiculous and unworthy, as Sir Alec Douglas-Home found to his inconvenience in 1972. The Commission should also certainly be represented at all summit meetings of the Nine. The President of the Council might, for the time being, be, according to the Belgian plan, elected for a year. The Council, still comprising the foreign ministers (or, on minor occasions, their deputies, such as the permanent representatives of the members when in Brussels), should have, as its main function over the next few years, the gathering together of as much power as the Community feels that it needs, and then prepare to hand over that power to those whom the European parliament, with the Commission, selects as the main authority. For example, if the President of the Commission and the Commissioners were nominated or elected by the parliament, perhaps from among their members, we should be going some way towards the formation of a European parliamentary government, and we could entertain the thought that the Council, its work of the first ten or twenty years in the Community being over, might then turn back slowly into a European senate, perhaps organized much as at present, or perhaps with its membership expanded – a senate which could articulate the continuing interests, desires, and drives of nations. Doubtless this senate should house permanent senators rather than, exclusively, men who, as foreign or finance ministers, are in Brussels from time to time: and perhaps the President of the Council might remain, along the lines of the constitution of the Roman Republic, a second, or parallel, source of authority in some matters. Such a development should not, also, prevent the achievement, if it were considered desirable, of a Chamber of Regions, to reflect the needs of peripheral and poor places within the Community, for the obsolete nation states are of course not the same as the resurgent regions. Although it may seem that some of these ideas are absurdly Utopian, such an attitude seems too modest. The next generation probably will regard these problems as easily overcome, and will marvel that they were ever regarded as serious impediments to progress.

The Council is served by a committee of permanent representatives, set up under an article of the Treaty of Rome 'to prepare the work of the Council and to carry out the tasks entrusted to it by the latter'. It carries out the essential task of sorting out the Council agenda into what shall be discussed and what shall be accepted without discussion. The Committee acts as a link between the national bureaucracies, and is a centre of liaison and information. It has undoubtedly eroded some of the Commission's influence. Like the Council, it is inevitably undemocratic, rather more so, in fact, since its members are not even national parliamentarians. Sometimes, the permanent representatives act as if they were the foreign ministers' deputies. Nobody, except the foreign minister concerned, is in a position to criticize the permanent representative, nor to question his work.

At the time of Britain's first application to join the Community the Commission already seemed the most powerful supranational body in the world. Since the Commission is responsible for initiating proposals for action by the Council of Ministers, it is more than an executive, and also less, since, except in a fairly restricted sense, it is not responsible for the carrying into effect of Community policy (that being done by governments, using their own resources). The Commission can indict member states and firms of the Community before the European Court for failing to carry out a clause of the Treaty of Rome or a decision of the Council of Ministers. It can issue directives and regulations (the latter being specific instructions to member states, the former being general rules the details of which are left to the states to carry out). Already, many countries have diplomatic representatives to it, and it too has modest diplomatic missions. Members of the Commission are appointed by all the governments in concert, though, once sworn in, they have had to assume extra-national status. The thirteen Commissioners (nine before Britain's entry), are, too, difficult to remove: singly, only, in fact, by the European Court, acting on a petition from the Council or the other members of the Commission; or, as a bloc, by a two-thirds majority of the European parliament. Neither procedure has yet been used. At the moment, the Council of Ministers rarely acts without a proposal from the Commission, though, it may be added, it does not act much anyway. During the Gaullist era the Commission lost some of its position, and its nerve. The Committee of permanent representatives moved onto the scene, and began to replace part of the Commission's executive role. Governments too have nominated people to the Commission who are more civil servants than independent politicians. It is doubtful whether the increase in the numbers of the Commissioners from nine to thirteen now that Britain is to join the EEC was beneficial: but, probably, there will not be a change in the numbers of the civil servants working in the Commission itself. (That, incidentally, is about one per cent of the number in the present British civil service, and much less than some single departments of state.)

The five different functions of the Commission have been analyzed as, first, *normative*, that is, the Commission's role in promoting the community interest and acting as guardian of the Treaty of Rome; *initiative*, that is, its activity in instigating legislation; *administrative*, a self-explanatory adjective; and *mediative*, that is, its role in attempting to achieve a compromise in, for example, a dispute in the Council. The first of these two activities are those which give the Council its originality, the last two are activities typical of first a normal national bureaucracy and, second, a normal international bureaucracy, such as

OECD. Fifthly, there is the important role of the Commission whereby it acts as 'watchdog of the Treaty' and take governments to court. Among these undertakings, the *mediative* role is crucial, and much more so than it would be in a typical international secretariat.

Now, there are several ways, some simple, some not, whereby the Commission could, and should, be improved: for example, the European parliament might relieve it of some preoccupations. The parliament's budgetary committee, for example, might take over some financial activities. Etienne Hirsch, ex-president of Euratom, in 1967 summed up the two main problems of the Commission as, first, the potential disintegratory consequences of making it easy for national administrations to second their officials to the European institution, thus either making them national spies in an international body or, at least, putting a strain on their loyalties. The second problem was that of balance between nations: 'It is obviously right that a balance should be sought in the composition of the body of officials except for those who are mostly recruited on the spot ... But this has crystallized into such a rigid form that every post of director general or of director has become the fief of a particular nation. It needs an incredible effort to replace a German by a Dutch director general. Things even threaten to go further. I came up against very strong objections when a Flemish Catholic Belgian was replaced in the post of director general by another Belgian but who was a socialist and a Walloon. Clearly', Monsieur Hirsch added, 'in these conditions one cannot make the most suitable choices', and he went on to complain that the opportunities for promotion are limited by considerations of nationality, which hamper the advance of those who would hope, by reason of their deserts, to make careers in the service, and discourage the best.

These are details, but serious matters, all the same, and need urgent consideration, particularly since the recruitment of new blood into the Commission from the three new countries will give a good opportunity for general replanning.

It should also be seen that a 'functionalist' approach to the Commission is, in the long run, an uncreative and, from a

European point of view, possibly even a dangerous, one. For the Commission has largely been constructed out of national officials seconded to Brussels, it being left to chance whether or not the men and women concerned are inspired with the European ideal. Even if they are, and they do their best to create the new Europe through the weight of institutional development and of precedent, they are many of them liable to return to work for national governments. In this sense they are European only insofar as the national context allows it. Despite the energy with which certain commissioners have tried to articulate, through their own will power, the European idea, the Commission has still no political basis of its own.

Taken all in all, however, the status of the Commission is extraordinary. Its fourth (but most unfortunately alas only temporary) President, Dr Sicco Mansholt, in a series of powerful and morally decisive speeches, attempted to do for Europe what Hammarskjöld tried to do to the UN. His remarks on the environment and conservation,* alluded to later, were a most inspiring statement. His rebuke to Mr Wedgwood Benn in the spring of 1972 over the Labour party's apparent change of mind over Europe was a powerful assertion of supranational authority. So was his indictment of the Greek regime in May 1972, after the banishing of Professor Pesmazoglou to a remote village. (That Professor was the distinguished economist who had negotiated Greece's association to the Common Market.) The same month, Dr Mansholt twice visited Santiago de Chile in order to attempt to persuade the countries of the less developed world at the UNCTAD conference that the Community had been misrepresented as a greedy and introverted rich group. He also made a powerful and committed endorsement of *Ostpolitik* at a meeting of the European movement in the German Bundestag during the crucial time of ratification. Whatever happens to the Commission and to the Community after January 1973 (and it is clear that a French President of the Commission will take over) the era of Mansholt will be regarded

* See below page 159.

always as one giving the most vigorous moral leadership to Europe.

The best approach to the problem of the future of the Commission is to link it directly with the parliament, and to require the commissioners to be invested by the parliament. This does not involve any amendment of the treaties. It needs an agreement between the governments that, prior to the definite appointment of the Commission, they will wait for the investiture of the proposed Commission by the European parliament. The Commission has itself proposed that, at the beginning of its term of office, it should present its programme to the European parliament and to the Council, indicating its priorities and their budgetary consequences. Important legislation should come back to the parliament for a second reading. If the Council diverges 'in a noteworthy way' from a proposal by the Commission, the parliament should at least have the chance of expressing its views on the Council's decision. The Commission also has suggested that the Council should go over to normal voting and should permit abstentions. Also, the Commission wants the parliament, by 1973, to have the right of co-decision in all measures of a legislative nature and has proposed that at least by 1980 the European parliament should be elected by direct suffrage.

The British, traditionally law-abiding, may be likely to take the regulations of the Commission more seriously than the governments of the Continent have done. For the Commission has produced an immense variety of draft Regulations, some of which have not been carried out. Governments have not wished to harmonize standards, or practice, as fast as the Commission has desired. But in Britain it seems probable that a regulation, however disagreeable, will be treated as law. For this reason alone, Britain will probably become very quickly the most European of European nations and, by taking regulations seriously, perhaps help to improve both them and the reality of the institution whose task is to frame them.

In May 1972 the Council of Ministers, with the British present (and the other members elect) agreed that it was desirable to set up a 'political secretariat', as a 'useful addition to the Community'. The decision was only reached after a quarrel with the Commission whose representatives some members of the Council sought to exclude. No decision was reached as to whether this should be set up in Paris, as was desired by the French, or in Brussels, as is logical, and desired by all other governments in the Community, including Britain. It was an idea apparently buried by the time of the Paris summit.

There is a sense in which the arguments about this secretariat are critical for the whole future of the Community. It is obvious that the French government, and perhaps the British government too, desire this to be an intergovernmental secretariat, not an international one. 'A secretariat for political cooperation,' Monsieur Pompidou has called it. That would mean that it would be staffed presumably only by regular national civil servants, and be outside the inspiration of the Commission. This would be a serious mistake. Unless politics is given the old-fashioned definition of being concerned primarily with foreign policy, the Commission can be regarded as already a major political body. If it is thought necessary at all, the political secretariat should be a full institution of the Community; or, at the least, it should be a body under a suitable secretary general responsible only to the Council and not to any individual minister.

The siting is undoubtedly important. To suggest, however, that it should be set up in France ignores the fact that the Community is already split up between Brussels, Luxembourg and Strasbourg. These splits mean less than they might have done a generation ago. Still, a French venue would make for further complication. This geographical matter will be discussed again. The French desire reflects not only, of course, national pride but, presumably, the belief that, by siting such a thing in their territory, they could keep it thinking confederally rather than federally, and reduce its European flavour generally. The proposal should be vigorously resisted.

There are several other institutions within the EEC which also need consideration. First of these is the Economic and

25

Social Committee. This is an attempt to bring workers together with employers, which has, as yet, had little effect. Its 101 members (economic and social advisers drawn from various sectors in the economic life of the Community) have inspired little enthusiasm in French workers and socialists, for example. The whole idea may easily smack too much of the Fascist Corporate state for everyone's comfort – or perhaps of the French 'plan'. There are twenty-seven employers, thirty-four workers and forty 'other interests'. The members devote a third of their time to their work for the Community, and give opinions to other institutions of the Community (the Council or Commission) which, however, do not have to heed them, though they have to consult the committee before making decisions in the economic or social field. These 'opinions' have ranged from general views, on how the Community is going, to health precautions. On the other hand, though ineffective as yet, the Committee does represent an attempt of sorts to try and devise new institutions rather than to repeat all the old ones with all their faults. There is considerable advantage in consulting the two sides of industry and other groups interested; it is even essential to planning in a mixed economy, and particularly one which is bound to contemplate some kind of scheme for workers' participation in decision-making.

Admittedly, the powers of the present Committee are not adequate. There would be a strong case for increasing them, including obligatory consultation on all issues. It might even be that the Economic and Social Committee could develop into a third chamber in a future European federation, with the same rights to initiate legislation as the other chambers. For a tricameral parliament might very well have more to it than would seem at first sight. The Paris communiqué limited the Community institutions to recognize the right of the ESC to advise on its own initiative on all questions affecting the Community.

This Committee will, after 1 January 1973, have 153 members of which twenty-four will come from Britain.

Other committees have similarly been developed: these include the Short and the Medium Term Economic Policy

Committees; the monetary and budgetary policy committees; the Committee of Governors of Central Banks; and the Transport Committee. There was also the possibility that, under the Werner Report's plan for monetary union, an 'Economic-policy decision-making body' would be developed which, in the end, would take over considerable responsibility for economic and social policy. All these committees, it should perhaps be borne in mind, are staffed by civil servants, not by the diverse groups represented in the Economic and Social Committee.

The European Court of Justice has hitherto comprised seven judges; after 1973, it will number eleven. It has worked adequately until now, within the narrow limits given to it, of adjudicating in disputes concerning the application either of the treaty or of the decisions of the Council, and, on the whole, governments or firms which have been fined by it, or called upon to refrain from practices illegal under one or other of the European treaties, have acted in accordance with the Court's injunction.

The Paris summit made little progress on institutions. The communiqué called for a report before the end of the first stage of the Economic and Monetary Union on 'the measures relating to the competences and responsibilities among the Community institutions'. The communiqué also advised holding (national) cabinet meetings on the same day, and called for 'practical steps' to impose the Parliament. But there was an understandably well publicized call for 'European Union' by 1980. A report was called for on this by 1975. This is quite encouraging. The Foreign Ministers of the Community were also to meet four times a year.

3 The European Parliament

At present, the European parliament, established in 1958 as the successor to the Common Assembly of the Coal and Steel Community, is not a legislature in the usual sense of the word. Its powers are no greater than were those of the Duma, the Russian parliament, before 1914: 'Members of the Duma,' Hugh Seton Watson tells us, 'might put questions to the prime minister or individual ministers, but they were not obliged to give satisfactory replies.'[10] The parliament does not form a government, and it has never even used its formal power to dismiss (by a two-thirds majority) the Commission – a power which is, at present, absurd, in the sense that it would be most improbable if it could politically ever be exercised. After all, it could not appoint a new Commission if it did so act. Members of the European parliament are, at the moment, delegated annually by the national parliaments and, at best, see themselves as a democratic opposition to the Council, and, therefore, are more a reaction to authority than an authority itself. The Council of Ministers are not responsible to the parliament and it is, of course, it which, at the moment, as representative of the states, makes decisions. The parliament may propose amendments to the budget proposed every autumn by the Commission, but it cannot oblige the Commission to accept the amendments concerned. The only qualification is that, from 1975, the parliament will have power over the Commission's administrative budget – but that is only $150M out of the Community's total budget of $3,000M. British entry into the EEC, with the other two candidate countries, will increase the size of the parliament

28

from 142 to 198 members; but it will not by itself do anything more. Yet the questions of how British parliamentarians are to be elected and what powers they should ultimately have, or seek, are of critical importance; and the discussion about that will probably inspire continental Europeans to consider the problem more carefully, since the British have been, on the whole, successful practitioners of parliamentary democracy.

Despite its absence of powers, the European parliament represents much more of a real assembly than, say, the formal assemblies of WEU, or NATO, or the Council of Europe. It is, in most ways, the most important institution of Europe's future, for its working will decide the crucial matter of whether or not Europe evolves a real democratic accountability. The tactical questions of the parliament's methods and procedure will closely affect the development of European democracy and whether a European constitutional treaty will be worked out. Most federations of the past have developed a two-chamber system as a means of balancing centrifugal and centripetal forces. But perhaps two chambers will seem either unnecessary, or inadequate: to chambers based on direct suffrage (either by proportional representation or by single member constituencies) and on regional interests (perhaps in the manner of the US Senate), there might, with advantage, as suggested earlier, be added a third chamber to represent capital and labour – or, at least, professional and industrial matters. Perhaps a fourth chamber should be considered too, to represent national interests. All these matters should be discussed and certainly the British political parties should develop their own ideas about them. But apart from the Anglo-Italian communiqué in the days of Harold Wilson's prime ministership, only two practical suggestions of a worthwhile kind have been made by leading English politicians on the Left: the proposals of Mr Michael Stewart, which are discussed later on, and Roy Jenkins' remark that he would 'like to see direct elections when – and not before – they would be likely to attract as high a poll as is normal in national elections'; and that remark was made in America.[11]

The next thing to be said is that there is more to this question than merely to insist that the Europe of the future is democratically organized; there are at least as many types of democracy as there are, for instance, supposed to be ways to socialism. Some democratic structures such as that of France during the Fourth Republic, have seemed unsatisfactory, as giving too much power to the legislature, and not enough to the executive. Some democratic assemblies, such as that of the Weimar Republic, have been misused to make democratic government impossible. Some systems such as that of the USA seem ideal on paper (and, indeed, for many generations did work well) but have become distorted because of the growth of government power. Within Europe at the moment there is wide variety of democratic practices – from the neglectful attitude towards the legislature of the Fifth Republic in France to the responsible one in Germany. In Britain, over the past generation, people have been consistently troubled about the power of the executive and the weakening of parliamentary control; about the growing power of the prime minister and of the Whips; all of which have combined to make governmental reform one of the most important but difficult of political matters and one which has been the least easy to achieve swift success, as the failure to reform the House of Lords has suggested.

There is the question of power and there is also the question of how these powers are best articulated. The response to these considerations is likely to be dictated by personal views of political or social priority: it is, however, easy to imagine how major foreign and defence problems could, over the next few years, be considered with 'Europe' providing a more effective way of achieving control than would be possible under the established democratic procedures of individual states. As will be seen later, the multi-national company is one such problem, as is the international institution; and, in the past twenty-five years, defence ministers of NATO have often taken decisions or initiatives which have been impossible for national parliaments to criticise or to modify effectively, since they have been alliance decisions.

The Treaty of Rome, in its Article 138, called on the

European parliament to make proposals for direct elections by a uniform procedure in all member states; and, in 1960, Monsieur Fernand Dehousse, a Belgian Socialist, drew up a scheme for this on behalf of the parliament of Europe, suggesting that the total number of seats should be raised to four hundred and twenty-six, the additional numbers to be filled by direct elections – each nation, for the time being, to decide for itself on the way of going ahead. Each parliament should last for five years. In the end, all seats were to be elected by a single method. But the Council of Ministers, under French delaying tactics, was unenthusiastic, so much so that, in 1969, the parliament even threatened to take the Council to the European Court for its laxity in complying with this article of the Treaty. Some work has gone on since then, though as yet inconclusively, and movements or individual politicians in all six countries have pledged themselves to the idea of direct elections – most suggesting that a single country might go ahead to secure this in respect of their own delegation even if Europe as a whole were to remain undecided. But nothing much has happened. The French government's opposition to direct elections to a working parliament derives primarily from the fact that France herself has a less than complete democracy. This means, of course, that it is not France, but the Gaullist regime, which the rest of Europe must regard as the stumbling block.

Now the subject has become alive again. A new report to the Commission has been prepared by fourteen men and women headed by Professor Georges Vedel, a French professor of constitutional law. (Andrew Shonfield, the new director of Chatham House, and Professor John Mitchell, of Edinburgh, were the British members.) This report concentrates on the powers of parliament rather than on its method of election. It suggests that to begin with, during a transitional period, the European parliament should have a power of 'co-decision' with the Council of Ministers on such matters as the revision of the founding treaties of the Community, the entry of new member states and the ratification of new international agreements. 'Consultation' of the parliament would also occur in respect of a variety of matters, such as the common farm policy, the harmonization of taxes, transport policy, the European Social Fund, foreign workers, mutual recognition of diplomas and the status of Community officials. 'Co-decision' would mean genuine concessions to the parliament's views, consultation would include the right to delay a decision of the Council for a month. Then, in 1978, a new stage might be reached. At that time, 'co-decision' would be extended to all the matters previously reserved to mere 'consultation', with the Commission specifically charged to mediate, if necessary.

The critical point about this committee's proposal is that it attempts to resolve what it rightly calls a vicious circle, whereby it has seemed pointless to extend the powers of the European parliament until the parliament genuinely represents something; and direct elections have seemed absurd unless the parliament has power. Professor Vedel and his friends make the clear judgment that the only way to escape from this dilemma is to proceed to give the parliament more power first (here differing from what was suggested in 1960). The Commission has prepared proposals based on the Vedel Report. It would be very desirable if the Labour party in Britain were to give its vigorous support to this realistic plan. This may seem to be to 'go ahead of public opinion'; but political parties are in duty bound to give leadership and direction to public opinion.

In May 1972, the Dutch government proposed that the countries of the Community should set a firm date by which time proposals for the direct elections for the European parliament should be made by the Council of Ministers. (The Commission, as noted earlier, has called for direct elections by 1980.) The Dutch government has also suggested that the parliament should be able to take decisions on proposals of the Commission if the Council procrastinates longer than a certain time – the Council in turn being able to object to the parliament's decision within a similarly agreed period. Now, in reply, Monsieur

Pompidou has made several rather dismissive comments about the activities of small nations: but, of course, small countries can perfectly well articulate general desires and widely held feelings even among the peoples of the larger countries. That is certainly the case in this particular respect.

As for the method of electing parliamentarians to the European assembly, Mr Michael Stewart and Sir Tufton Beamish have made suggestions, separately, for methods of direct election to European parliaments of members who would also have the right to sit in national ones. Mr Stewart proposes direct elections of European parliamentarians, from large constituencies, at the same time as national ones; Sir Tufton proposes an election of alternate members, who would serve in the national parliaments when the European member is away. Mr Stewart's parliamentarians would automatically also be members of national parliaments and could vote by proxy.[12] The argument is complicated; Professor Vedel's scheme would maintain for the time being the importance of national parliaments, thereby placing a strain, an intolerable strain, perhaps, upon English parliamentarians – if Strasbourg remains the venue for the parliament. It is impossible, also, to see how real democratic accountability can be secured by anything short of direct elections, as the Anglo-Italian declaration on the subject suggested in April 1969 – the late Labour government's most forward-looking document on this matter – on the occasion of an official visit to Britain of President Saragat and Pietro Nenni, then foreign minister: 'Europe must be firmly based on democratic institutions, and the European communities must be sustained by an elected parliament, as provided for in the Treaty of Rome.' Others in the course of 1972 have made further interesting proposals. Mr David Steel, for example, has suggested that the European parliamentarians from Britain should, temporarily, become peers.

This subject might be approached gradually: direct elections might affect only half the seats to begin with, the rest being nominated. We must hope, however, that neither main party in

33

Britain will allow, or allow each other to allow, that the British parliamentarians should be merely representatives nominated by the existing parliamentary parties at Westminster. The advantages of Mr Stewart's proposal is that it would create immediately strong political personalities whose loyalties would be to regions and large areas of economic, social and political importance.

There are many other problems: what if direct elections to the European parliament gave an 'anti-European' majority? How exactly can the European parliament be given those powers which can make Europe a real democratic undertaking? Would it really be desirable for the President of the Commission to be appointed by the parliament? Or the whole Commission? And should the President select the Commission, or should perhaps he or they ideally be directly elected? And exclusively from members of the parliament, as with the British prime minister? Should we really hope that the Council might become a senate to represent regional interests or 'national' ones? What will happen to those other semi-legislative bodies, such as the consultative assembly of the Council of Europe, the assembly of the Western European Union, and the unofficial assembly of NATO parliamentarians? There are detailed questions, too, of numbers of seats, methods of voting, and length of parliament, conditions of work, which, in practice, turn out to be of importance. How many members are an ideal number for a working legislature of a community as large as Western Europe?

As for the solution, the most radical one is, as so often, the most intelligent, both in respect of power and of composition: namely, that a democratically elected European parliament of largely full-time European parliamentarians should select the President of the Commission by proposal, objection and appointment, and the Commissioners as well. The most important part, as most people have rightly pointed out, recalling doubtless lessons of constitutional history, is that the parliament ought, as soon as possible, to be endowed with real powers. Less important, perhaps, are the other questions, such as whether or

34

no the parliamentarians would be directly elected from the start. But it would be wrong to be content with that for long: a career in European politics would be different, and should be allowed to be different, from (though not necessarily superior to) one in national politics. For the problem of dealing, at the same time, with two separate legislatures taxes the physique of the toughest; it leads to the neglect of one or other of the two institutions – perhaps both – excessive travelling, incessant upheavals and a home life incapable of offering the tranquillity necessary for wise political decisions. These difficulties have already been encountered even by members of the existing European parliament. One commentator has written correctly: 'It has become less and less possible for national MPs who attend the European parliament to keep up a regular attendance at their national assembly and, at the same time, be active European members. Increasingly, they have been faced with a choice. . .'[13] Already European parliamentarians are expected to be present for one hundred sessions, about thirty-seven days a year, plus committees, from March until August, and this is certain to be expanded. With travelling, it can take up to one hundred days a year. These difficulties would be greater still for British parliamentarians.

Several new points should be made: first, in the interests of stability, the European parliament, and its election arrangements, might be so institutionally (even architecturally) organized as to favour the growth of majorities; secondly, this might be met by some form of procedural law whereby, for example, votes of no confidence were dependent (as in German and in British practice) upon the certainty of being able to form a new government; thirdly, the parliament should not be so large as to prevent the development of strong political personalities, able to react vigorously against the intolerable demands of a whipping system such as currently disfigures British parliamentary practice. One of the reasons why the hundred or so senators in the US are such strong influences, for good or evil, is that there are so few of them. For this reason

35

any great extension in the number of parliamentarians in the European parliaments of the future might be an error : thirty-six, the number currently suggested for Britain, might be more than enough.

The 198 members of the European Parliament will, from 1 January 1973, comprise 36 members from Britain, France, Germany and Italy, 14 each from Belgium and the Netherlands, ten from Denmark and Ireland, and six from Luxembourg. Some criticism must attach to this arrangement, since it is obvious that Luxembourg, a chance creation of the nineteenth century, has a disproportionate power. In fact, chance developments of that sort probably will have a beneficial effect, at least in these next stages of the development of the Community.

It has several times naturally been suggested, here and elsewhere, that the interests of different groups or interests within a federated Europe could be most easily articulated by means of a two-chamber system: but the relation between two chambers has rarely been effectively balanced, with one or the other being more powerful in practice. It might very well be that a single large chamber with different chapters within it might be the most promising : thus the one hundred and ninety-eight members of the parliament in January 1973 might be supplemented, within their own walls, by specifically regionalist or industrialist members. (Historians of parliament such as Mr Enoch Powell will recall the diversity of late mediaeval legislative assemblies and be comforted perhaps by finding they have descendants in contemporary proposals.)

Within the European parliament, already, and in the WEU and Council of Europe assemblies, parties from different countries have collaborated. Already, and from the beginning, those who sat in the European parliament have sat not in alphabetical order of state round the hemicycle but in supranational political groups. They will collaborate increasingly, though sympathy between European Christian democracy and English Conservatives is obviously more difficult, because of the confessional element in the former's ideas, than that between socialists: an additional advantage of the Community from the latter's point in view, one would have thought.

It has always indeed seemed likely that, from the point of view of tactics, the Left has a better chance of achieving an effective working alliance than the Right in a European parliament. As earlier suggested, socialists are, by definition, more internationalist than Conservatives. The social democratic parties of Europe, Britain included, share a common approach, even though Marx plays a bigger part in the outlook of continental socialists than in that of ours. So, of course, too do the communists, though they are, at the moment, more divided than any other group. Yet, partly because of the divisions in the British Labour movement, the Conservatives and Christian Democrats – not the easiest of allies – have had a head start in European consultation. The growth of European parties may nevertheless be the critical development of the future, of greater importance perhaps than the more carefully analyzed and more predictable institutions of the community which are, after all, potentially artificial. Parties genuinely organized on the European scale would be in a far better position to judge problems of pollution, migrant workers, and multinational companies – evidently among the real political problems of the next ten years – than ones which are narrowly national in character. In this respect, Gerda Zellentin, a German constitutional scholar at the Institute for Political Science and Research at the University of Cologne, made a careful analysis of the behaviour of the parties within the European parliament during its first years, and reached the conclusion that the socialists were 'not only the largest group but that as a parliamentary group they show the strongest cohesion'.[14] A study of voting behaviour revealed that, among the European parliamentarians, 'the socialists are actually the only force whose long range dominant goal is the establishment of an economic and political European community'. Thus the socialist opposition within the parliament developed into what another German scholar, O. Kirchheimer, has referred to as 'the auxiliary engine' of the integration of

Europe. The socialist group, for example, has asked far more questions than any other party within the parliament.*

There is an additional point to be made about direct election, and that is that, in most national parliaments, the space allocated to the independent member and even to smaller parties is scant indeed. The European parliament should avoid this weakness. The independent member, and the independent minded member of an established party, have played a useful part in the life of national parliaments – not perhaps in the main stream of political life, but in the scarcely less important matter of tolerance for deviant behaviour. In Britain, we owe to Sir Gerald Nabarro the Clean Air Bill, to Sir Alan Herbert the Divorce Act of 1937, to Sidney Silverman, probably, the abolition of capital punishment, to David Steel the Abortion Act, and to several other such independent-minded members, such as Leo Abse, the Homosexual Relations Bill. The present whipped system in England demands too much of the patience, capacity for abnegation and self-control of members. Criticism of democracy has always, and almost uniquely, depended upon criticism of party politics; but individual members have often been the glory of democracies.

*WRITTEN QUESTIONS FROM 1958 TO 1965–6
(CLASSIFIED BY POLITICAL GROUPS):

	Christian Democrats	Socialists	Liberals	UNR–UDT	Total
1958	10	14	1	4	29
1959–60	31	41	12	–	89
1960–1	40	73	43	–	156
1961–2	24	66	13	–	103
1962–3	56	117	19	–	192
1963–4	59	79	22	6	166
1964–5	47	98	20	1	166
1965–6	32	87	13	2	134
TOTAL	299	575	143	13	1030

Source: Secretariat of the European Parliament 1966, compiled by Gerda Zellentin.

These and similar difficulties might be avoided by altering the system of election: of, for example, moving over towards proportional representation, and possibly even using the system of the single transferable vote, such as used in Ireland and in many minor undertakings in Britain. Proportional representation is used in seven of the Community's parliamentary systems. The English constituency system may have deep roots in the English past. But, if the constituencies in a European parliament are to be as big as they will have to be, it is doubtful whether this old principle could be successfully transferred; and it is doubtful too whether the system could be transplanted with the success that has on the whole characterized it in Britain.

There is another and perhaps determining argument: the single member seat exaggerates the support for large parties, in the interests of political stability. This justification, however, is only of recent date, since the party system is itself only of recent origin and the British system, in its modern form, still enshrines the era of the independent-minded private member, perhaps sponsored by a great landlord, perhaps not, but, at all events, not owing allegiance to a single (if usually inconsistent) ideology. The consequence may have helped the stability of the system, but it has also helped to fossilize it. It has led to the neglect of powerful minority groups, and even driven them to seek satisfaction, or to contemplate it, outside the democratic system. This affects all the main three regional groups. If proportional representation had been introduced earlier, the disastrous events in Northern Ireland of the late 1960s and 1970s might have been avoided. The existing system in Britain has led to myths, as well as to inequities: and the former are even more dangerous than the latter. One myth is that 'Wales is Socialist', when Labour, in 1970, gained only 48 per cent of the vote; and another is that the South of England, outside London, is all proudly True Blue. But the Conservatives, in 1970, gained only 53 per cent of the vote, though they got most of the seats. One might also compare the size of the Liberal vote in Britain, and that of the Free Democrats in Germany, and note the politically important part played by the latter and the impotent one played by the former – to the loss, as any fair-minded person would admit, of the whole community. Finally, the transfer of our system to Europe might risk the formation of national or regional blocks, and would certainly discourage the formation of transnational parties, which are essential for future integration. In the long run, proportional representation across the whole of Europe would certainly lead to the disintegration of frontiers, which is a good in itself.

It could be, too, that the single member system would result in the total exclusion from full integration of several whole political manifestations such as the British Liberals, or the French Socialists, or the Communist party in countries other than France and Italy.

The parliamentary system to be created should also avoid, by means of built-in safeguards of one sort or another, the mistakes of existing parliaments in the nation states. When reading the speeches of Michael Foot or of Enoch Powell it sometimes sounds as if everyone should feel satisfied with the parliaments as they now are: whereas it is clear that these institutions have shortcomings. In England, for example, the system has scarcely changed since the days of the stage coach, when distance alone made it inevitably difficult for members of parliament to be truly in touch with their constituencies. Government has also today so many facets that legislation often presents the appearance of a most wearing series of incomprehensible regulations.

Is this a plan for national parliaments to sink to the level of county councils or land assemblies? The answer partly depends on the tone in which it is put. For, within the next generation, central governments will probably seem too ponderous and too remote for the articulation of many current desires: public participation in local government, or local government issues, is increasing; and, perhaps, in the future, we shall speak of the parish pump without the scorn implicit in the phase heretofore, and which would certainly not have grown into such invidious currency in France or in Germany.

Nevertheless we should remember that, in the lucid phrase of Professor Christoph Sasse of Cologne, 'Political leadership and democratic legitimization are interdependent. We shall, in fact, not take the Community seriously until it is democratic, since the democratic nation state will, until then, seem a more just undertaking, despite its failures.'[15] Direct elections will, by themselves, increase the possibilities of political power, since people will take more seriously a body which has been elected; and the emergence of a vigorous European parliament is naturally essential (according to the democratic ideals in which most of us believe) to the business of creating a European federation.

4 The Challenge of the Institutions

Farsighted decisions upon the matters discussed in the previous two chapters, in particular on the general one of securing a political direction to the whole enlarged Community, will affect European and, presumably therefore, world, history decisively. Several extra matters need also to be mentioned. It should be established, for example, that, if there should ever be a senior executive politician, or 'President', of Europe, it should be so arranged that there would be no chance either of the prolonged electioneering which distorts US politics for so long beforehand (and often causes political decisions to be taken, or left untaken, for as much as a year beforehand specifically for electoral reasons), or of such a president remaining in power for a long time. We should look carefully indeed for inspiration at political systems such as modern Switzerland, or at the Roman Republic, where supreme power is limited to particular people for short periods. Britain, after all, has been full of people who might have made good prime ministers but have never had the chance because of the long-term, life-time (as it often seems), dominance of single limpet-like leaders. This point was recently put by the new Secretary General of the Italian Communist Party, Enrico Berlinguer: 'Over supper in L'Aquila, Signor Enrico Berlinguer, the Communist leader, confessed that the secretary-ship which he has just inherited is a heavy load. Elections apart, he cannot see how his family life will escape the strain. He said he was toying with the idea of a revolving secretaryship. He thought the party mature enough now to allow its supreme post to pass from hand to hand so that one man would hold it for a period of years, not for life.'[16] Perhaps the European Labour, Christian Democrat, liberal and Conservative parties will soon be similarly mature.

An acceptance of this idea would prevent the prolonged and often distasteful arguments about personalities which distort much political writing. Politics would greatly profit from general disintoxication. Mention of the Roman Republic should cause us, too, to consider again, at least for a moment, the question whether the new Europe might not with advantage have two executive heads, like the Consuls. The idea of a single head to an institution derives from the family but the family is disintegrating and, in many modern families, decisions are joint, if not collective.

Another critical point to be made, and to be insisted upon at an early stage, relates to government or Community information. It is of fundamental importance, from the point of view of securing liberty in the future, that European institutions should not be allowed to create around themselves the arcana of secrecy and private confidence which have characterized governments of nation states during the last fifty years. Official Secrets Acts, of the type devised to meet the apparent threat of a German war in 1911, and then maintained, since it was convenient to governments in a host of other ways, should be rigorously eschewed. The right approach is obviously that of President Kennedy, who remarked that the communication of information was one of the most important activities of government. Kennedy was speaking, too, in a society where the absence of an Official Secrets Act of the English type has had one obvious and beneficient consequence: namely, the ability of serious journalists to comment upon, with an informed mind, governmental policies before decisions are taken. Occasionally, this has led to inconvenience, and even rage, on the part of government officials. But there can be few occasions when, looking back, it can really be said that government has been hindered by this more open and self-confident procedure. Even the scandals that have been caused have often been of great service to the community: this has also had a beneficient

43

consequence for journalism in the US and must be one of the main reasons for the high standard of commentators in the leading US papers. Civil Service anonymity is much less of an asset to effective government than used to be supposed, and, indeed, even the British government has made a number of concessions to this view. It is difficult enough to get a story right in journalism without governments trying to make that impossible. This is more and more important as governments come to be responsible for more and more of the community's business.

The British slowness in moving towards a more open attitude is doubtless one more consequence of its twentieth-century good luck in avoiding the crash of prestige which attended all governmental undertakings on the continent in the 1940s. The British government has, on the whole, maintained its integrity, and nobody really believes that the practice of our government conceals untruth on a colossal scale – though there have been a number of little white lies. Governments should generally place themselves in the situation of journalists whose function, to communicate to the public a judicious but instantaneous appraisal of events, is so important, and so helpful to government in the long run, in a free society.

The question of where all this is to go on is also important. Can the parliament really be effective if it is established in Strasbourg, and the Commission in Brussels? It is even odder that the headquarters of the parliament should be in Luxembourg, along with the European Court. Or does this surprise suggest an old-fashioned prejudice that 'centres' are desirable? Might a divided centre of decision help the remoter regions? It is not at all proved. As it is, the distances between Brussels, Luxembourg and Strasbourg are just great enough to make journeys between them extremely disagreeable and complicated. To solve these problems, the *Economist* in June 1972 proposed the idea of a revolving parliament, to meet in the different capitals of the Community, thereby preventing the 'Europeans' from becoming a kind of group apart. *The Times* has proposed that Paris should be the headquarters of the parliament, so that it would become 'the political centre of the Community, Brussels the economic centre, and London the natural place for a commercial centre'. Meantime, there is Monsieur Pompidou's suggestion for a political secretariat to be established in France – forty kilometres outside Paris, as rumour has it, in an already designated place. An entirely new capital has also been suggested, a kind of European Brasilia, though where such an artificial creation might be is obviously a loaded question. It is difficult indeed not to suspect that President Pompidou's plan for a political secretariat in France is in itself a scarcely veiled suggestion that the capital of Europe should spring up as a new Versailles.

The essential point in this controversy, however, is that the institutions should all be in the same place. Where that is, is of less moment. A French site would be acceptable if it were certain that France would not attempt to profit overmuch from the arrangement and would abandon the Gaullist obstructionism of recent years. But of that, there seems no sign. By and large, Brussels is the best place for a European capital. It is the geographical centre of the new Europe of the Nine, and it is easy to get to. Belgium is not a country with an overwhelming national past. The Grand' Place would be a worthy and appropriate heart to Europe. Such psychological symbolism as would pertain to Belgium, as the occasion for the expansion of the First World War or the recollection of the manner of Belgium's creation in 1830, would be salutary. Belgian nationalism is not strong, and, as it is, the country may divide one day between Walloons and Flemings. In such circumstances, Brussels, and Brabant, could easily develop into a European federal district, which would, of course, include the battlefield of Waterloo, the most important battle in European history. Luxembourg, meantime, might remain the centre of the European Court of Justice, its relative remoteness being perhaps an encouragement to calm, judicial decisions.

It could be that, given a desire for it, a 'United States of Europe' could turn into a community of rapacious capitalism; or a community where superstition or religion were allowed free rein, under a reactionary Catholic lead; or one where, in alliance with the Soviet Union, the freedom of the individual was sacrificed in the supposed long-term interests of the majority. But from the character of the institutions already created, in particular the Commission; from the nature of the desires of the more enterprising 'Europeans'; and from the trend of events within Europe since 1957, the prevailing mood will probably be what most would describe as 'democratic socialist'. An undogmatic socialism, to be sure, similar to the ideology-free socialism of the *entente* powers during the First World War; and, as yet, a non-institutional democracy. But democratic socialist, just the same, in that, while it would be unthinkable to most working Europeans not to try and secure common policies within the Community, broadly in the general interest, it would be equally unthinkable for any to contemplate a denial of personal liberty. At least one English socialist, Roger Evans of the Society for Labour Lawyers, has recognized the Treaty of Rome, now signed by the British Conservative government, as a 'perfectly adequate political framework for the achievement of a socialist future'. Some of the arguments put forward by opponents of the Common Market from the heart, as it has seemed, of the Labour movement, recall oddly the complaints which used to be made in the late 1940s about the 'creeping bureaucracy' of the 'men from Whitehall': witness Jack Jones's complaints, at the Common Market Conference in 1971, about the tachograph, the 'spy in the cab' which will be compulsory in all western European commercial vehicles after 1978. We should remember we will be joining a Europe of Nine, not a Europe of Six; and, in Denmark and Holland, as well as in England, the Labour movements are well established and are experienced champions of democratic socialism against both Left and Right wing extremism, or totalitarian temptations. One of the fundamental points of the Treaty of Rome is the obligation to member states to seek the 'constant improvement of the living and working standards of their peoples'; and, finally, we should recall that, as Professor Swann has put it (in his *The Economics of the Common Market*), 'If Britain seeks to minimize her political commitment, she may also minimize her economic advantages.'

5 The US, Britain and Europe

The cohesion of a community is decided by the face it shows to the outside world. Thus, the likely unity of the European nations can be guessed at most easily from what organization exists for its relation with the exterior; and, as yet, though Presidents of the Commission, by the nature of their office, have exerted diplomatic power, and other institutions within the Commission have used diplomatic presence, the only explicit Community institution is the body set up as a result of the Davignon Report. The purpose of that is specifically limited to relations with countries other than those of the Community, co-ordination of diplomatic matters (for example, diplomatic recognition), and common policies in existing international organizations. This is not very ambitious and one, favourable, commentator has suggested that the Concert of Europe established in the post-Napoleonic period had got as far.[17]

The most critical aspect of the foreign politics of the Community is its relationship with the USA. This is paradoxical, since the desire to escape from US economic, technological and political dominance was undoubtedly one of the drives making for European unity. The US is still western Europe's military ally, and really her protector, and no one can say what would happen if that protection were either to be withdrawn completely or to be made to seem less credible, *in extremis*. The military power of the US is, furthermore, based upon a huge investment in research and in advanced technology, whose peaceful consequences have given to US private companies a great stake, through subsidiaries, in the industries of Europe. These indus-

47

tries are, understandably, the very ones on which European countries are hoping to depend in the future for their own commercial eminence and prosperity. The US is thus much the largest single foreign investor in the Community, as in Britain. She has a coherent, important and solid private or bilateral relation with most of the countries of the Community, including Britain and Ireland. There are some products, such as enriched uranium, which at present only the US can provide to the Community and which Europe needs, for her nuclear power reactors. Despite the US political faltering in Asia, particularly of course Vietnam, and even in the USA itself, the likelihood too is that the US technological advantage will grow rather than . lessen, the international company seeming to US investors and managers a more and more attractive system of organization and of profit. Quite how far the US technological superiority will carry is debatable : economists, particularly left wing economists, disagree on the question as to what extent Japan and Europe will be able to rival the US, or be absorbed by it. There are also critical monetary problems between the Community and the USA, partly deriving from French fears of US 'dollar supremacy'. The US dislikes the CAP almost as much as Professor Kaldor does, since it plainly hinders the sale of US temperate foodstuffs to Europe. Finally, the US dislikes the Community's association agreements and trade preference agreements which she construes as being against the spirit and perhaps the letter of GATT.

At all events, some problems in the future will, no doubt, occur between the US and Europe. Senator McGovern, for example, based part of his campaign for the Presidency in 1972 on an appeal to the US government to bring US troops home from Europe as well as from Asia; and though campaigns are one thing and action is another, it is easy to imagine that one day, not tomorrow perhaps or the day after, but one day, the US will wish to cut to the bone, at least its open-ended commitment to defend Western Europe. It is also easy to imagine continuing commercial or monetary difficulties with the US, particularly if the Commission's actions against multinational companies in Europe (and many 'multinational' companies are US-based) take on an anti-US flavour. Finally, a Europe anxious to assert its unity could easily try and suggest an independence in foreign policy which may be spurious at the time, but which may, nevertheless, be disintegratory. De Gaulle's foreign policy had material consequences, even though it consisted really only of gestures. What will happen too, if the lower cost of Japanese and European goods really causes a serious crisis in the US?

Thus, in considering the US, we are considering the real, as opposed to the mythical, side of European unification. In doing so, too, we have to remember that, for Britain, the most likely real alternative to a policy of joining the Community would have been to enter into a closer, and, culturally, politically and economically more subservient, friendship with the US. The attitude of the British to the US over the last quarter century has resembled that of left wing employees on the newspapers of Lord Beaverbrook: we have taken the money of the US, her military protection, but we have complained *sotto voce*, and made jokes at the US expense to salve our troubled consciences. Similarly, Britain's 'special relationship' with the US, and the fact of the common language, will obviously affect the determination of European policy, perhaps beneficiently (as Roy Jenkins seemed to think likely in his recent lectures at Yale in 1971), perhaps not. The nineteenth-century association between Britain and the US, when Britain was responsible for much of US economic development, has, of course, led to a close and continuing economic association in the twentieth, quite apart from all political considerations. We must also bear in mind that the power of the US since 1945 has been such that European powers have really done little against her wishes, singly or collectively. Suez, the one act of defiance, failed precisely because of US opposition. Furthermore, only a fool would deny that the role of the US in European affairs since 1945 has often been beneficial. The Marshall Plan was, undoubtedly, 'an act of farsighted generosity', even though it also had the political intention of encouraging European co-operation, which

49

Americans hoped would prevent any third European war. Despite the evils of modern America, of which the world has been made only too aware, American society is, in many ways, still more experimental, socially conscious and intellectually alive than the old world. Europe's relations with the US since 1945 have never been entirely dominated by anti-communism, and the USA has usually been enthusiastic about the idea of British membership of the Community. Still, the political circumstances of dependence on the US have seemed to be disagreeable to many, and rightly. It is also possible that the US may become entangled in new debilitating conflicts and tensions in Asia or Latin America in the future, or even within the US itself. No one wishes to be dragged into them, or even into a repetition of the thoughtless alignment which Britain took up with the USA during the Wilson government, primarily because of economic weakness.

The creation of a strong, self-confident, socially experimental and economically generous Europe will help to prevent the gradual Americanization of Britain and of Europe. A united Europe will be no political threat to the US; indeed, her attraction as an ally, and as an intermediary, perhaps as an enlightened friend, in a variety of crises or even wars, will be great. The possibilities of economic rivalry are considerable, but that is better than the alternative of US domination. The aim of statecraft in Europe must be to control such rivalry so that it does not risk political friendship or, for the forseeable future, military collaboration.

6 Britain, Europe and the World

After the US, the most complicated relationship which the Community will have is probably that with the other non-Community countries of Western Europe. Here, there is no single pattern, since there is no single existing relation. Spain, for example, desires an association with the Community, and in the long run to become a full member; at the moment, formally she is not a part of NATO, yet has an exceptionally close military alliance with the US. Portugal is in NATO but does not wish for membership of the Community. Switzerland and Austria have relations with the Community that are similar to each other, though the neutrality of each has a different basis—choice, tradition and economic self-sufficiency in the case of Switzerland, international status and relation with Russia in the case of Austria. Sweden and Finland, ex-members of EFTA like Switzerland and Austria, have similar motives for neutrality, though the possibility of Swedish adherence to the Community in the long run is considerable. Norway may join in the end after all. Greece and Turkey are associated with the Community and are supposed to become part of it by about 1984, though it is difficult to imagine how that will actually happen.

Greece, in this respect (although obviously not in others), looks more promising than does Turkey, which could only too easily find itself embarked, in the next few years, not upon integration with Europe but upon a prolonged civil war, in which class and secession are prominent (75 per cent of the 'Turkish People's Liberation Army' are apparently Kurdish). Similarly, Turkey's geographical position makes it undesirable that it should sever itself from its Arab and other neighbours. It also is obvious that the pattern of friendships, within Europe and without, will change with the entry of Britain and the other three candidates: the effect of three obviously non-Latin countries, and two leading Protestant ones, will have consequences for external relations as well as for internal ones.

The European Community countries' relations with Eastern Europe also differ, the Federal Republic's special relation with East Germany being, clearly, one obvious example. No association which Germans ever achieve with the rest of us in the West can be so close as that which they have, and, in some ways, now have more than ever (after the general treaty of traffic of May 1972), with each other. The German Social Democrats were, for years, critical of the European Community, not because they were bad Europeans but, in practice, because they disliked any policy which then seemed to them likely to prevent the reunification of Germany – a conclusion which no longer seems a consequence of the Community – indeed, the 'declaration by the Government of the Federal Republic of Germany covering the definition of German nationals' annexed to the Treaty of Rome means that theoretically East Germany is within the customs zone of the Community.

There is also the problem of Japan, which has already begun to pose a serious commercial challenge for Europe – Britain less than the continental countries as yet, but only for the moment. Japanese cars, systems of telecommunications, computers and aircraft, will soon be competitive in Europe. In 1971, Japanese exports were 25 per cent up on 1970, and in the first months of 1972 it was plain that a much larger increase was certain in that year – particularly in respect of Italy, where Japanese exports had increased 40 per cent over 1971 in the first few months. Meantime, the Community's trade to Japan's still protected market was actually 5 per cent lower in 1971. At the same time, Japan and the Community plainly have much in common, so far as their relation with US tariffs is concerned: the US has raised a high tariff against Japan's electronic equipment, and the Community will be expected to continue to protest against this – in the interest, no doubt, of avoiding the main thrust of Japanese exports, in the unstable days after the 'Nixon shock', as the Japanese call the US monetary measures of August 1971.

As for China, Chinese officials have usually made clear that they regard the Community as a stabilizing influence in the world, and especially as a counterbalance to the US and the Soviet Union. The growth of the Community has been called 'a grave obstacle' to the continued financial domination of the dollar, and the Chinese have spoken even enthusiastically of the Eurodollar as a desirable 'non-reserve currency'. The Community in 1970–1 was China's third most important trading partner, accounting for one-seventh of China's trade; once Britain and her colleagues are full members of the Community, the proportion will increase.

More important, and more intractable, is the Middle East, not, of course, because of Europe's old imperial connection with it, but for two reasons: Israel, and oil. Israel, with whom the Community has a preferential trading arrangement, similar to Spain's, is a European responsibility and with the fate of it all European countries are involved. The cynicism of Gaullism, the relative indifference of Mr Heath, the hostility of the well-intentioned, younger Left, should not prevent Israel from being a dominant charge on our preoccupations. Oil strikes closer to our direct interests: a regular and sustained flow of oil from the producing countries of the Middle East remains, and will remain for the forseeable future, of decisive importance, so much so that Ivor Richard and his colleagues, in their book *Europe or the Open Sea,* argued that 'the maximization of our influence over such areas of the world must therefore be one of the main objectives of our foreign policy' – and this fifteen years after Suez.[18] The point, however, has to be made: for the Community, unlike Russia and the USA, needs to import her main source of energy.* Here, Japan is in the same plight as ourselves.

One of the five conditions laid down by the National

* For the European energy problem in general, see page 154.

Executive of the Labour Party in 1962 for joining the EEC was 'fulfilment of the [Macmillan] government's pledge to our associates in the European Free Trade Area' – that is to the three Scandinavian countries, Finand, Iceland, Switzerland, Portugal and Austria. Now EFTA was a curious cause for the Labour party to take up so vigorously, since it had been, in fact, the compromise plan of Mr Maudling, when President of the Board of Trade in the late 1950s, for dealing with the commercial challenge of the community. It had, however, been welcomed by the Labour movement when it was first introduced, more as a *pis aller* than anything more elaborate.

EFTA had several advantages. In practice, less damage came as a result of the division of Europe into two trade areas than had been thought likely. In 1970, EFTA inhabitants both sold more to, and bought more from the rest of the world *per* head than did those of the Community or of the US.

But it was not large enough. Its future could only be to create commercial tension and tariff war with the Community, and weaken the Community's possibilities of political union. It was not everywhere popular. The papermakers of Britain hated it, as well they might, since the import of cheaper paper from Finland and Scandinavia had the effect of closing twenty-three paper mills and losing eight thousand jobs (in 1972, paper manufacturers in Britain were furious when it seemed that Britain's Common Market negotiators were more worried about the interests of Scandinavian manufacturers after January 1973 than the British). In 1972, the Community successfully negotiated with members of EFTA who were not candidates for EEC, Britain being active in EFTA's cause, and in late July the EEC and EFTA were formally merged: 20 per cent of the tariffs on industrial goods will be abolished each year for the five years after 1 April 1973, so that by 1978 EFTA and EEC will form a single industrial market. It seems that, by 1985, these ex-EFTA countries, with a considerable number of tariff cuts, will be either in the Community (Sweden and Norway are the most likely candidates and, after her, Austria) or (as is likely in the case of Finland and Switzerland for differing reasons), will be in effect the Community's associates. Already, for example, Switzerland has considered, and rejected (temporarily, perhaps), the proposal that she should associate with the proposed arrangements for currency of the Community. By the end of the 1970s, the main Swedish car plant, Volvo, will have half its manufacturing capacity situated outside Sweden. A sixteen-nation free trade area in industrial goods, embracing most of Western Europe, is really more likely than not by the end of the 1980s.

The effect of British entry into the EEC upon the Spanish political scene is likely to be considerable. Spain is linked with the Community by a preferential trade agreement which, over six years from 1970, will mean the reduction of tariffs by the Community on imports from Spain of 60 per cent for most products: Spain is reducing her tariffs by between 25 and 30 per cent. In 1976, another trade agreement is likely, cutting tariffs still more. But Spain trades extensively with Britain. In 1971, for example, Britain took 13 per cent of Spanish exports (£15M). This means that Spain will probably have to enter the Community in the long run, and will, therefore, presumably have to make some political concessions, if they are necessary. British entry, therefore, into the Community may be a major force for change in a country whose political structure has remained remarkably static during the last thirty years, despite its economic dynamism.

To the general surprise, this has been recognized by the Spanish Socialists who, in an unusual moment of concord, between the new Socialist party of the Interior (*Partido Socialista del Interior*, or PSI) and the old Socialist Party of exile and of the Republic (*Partido Socialista de Obreros Espanoles*, or PSOE), have issued a joint statement saying that 'they consider that the juridical-political situation with relation to a united Europe ... in which our country finds itself, is extremely harmful for the present and the future of Spain'. The statement continued: 'Unavoidable demands of an historical, cultural, social, political and economic nature' make Spain's eventual participation in the Community a necessity. On this point, the Spanish foreign minister, López Rodó, would doubtless agree with the socialists.

The economic case for Spain's association with, and ultimate entry into, the Community has been strong for some years, even though the jolt to the huge number of small undertakings in the country will be great. On the other hand, the economic growth in Spain in the last few years has been tremendous: silently and without fanfare, Spain has slipped past Britain to become the world's fifth largest shipbuilder, the second largest tourist country in the world, and so on. Nor is Spain now only, or even primarily, an exporter of a few old main products – fruit, vegetables, wine; 30 per cent of Spanish exports to Britain are now machinery and 'transport equipment', and manufactured goods account for 25 per cent of total exports.

At the same time, the political drawbacks to encouraging Spanish entry into the Community unless the regime becomes democratic are great. Opposition in Italy and the Benelux countries, not to mention Britain and Scandinavia, will be overwhelming. This is not specially obdurate, for all democratic Europeans desire to see an end to the authoritarian character of the present Spanish regime. It should also be obvious that the present regime in Spain would simply be unable to carry out many of the clauses of the Treaty of Rome (the regional policies, for example). Therefore, the progress of Spain towards democracy will probably proceed *pari passu* with her progress towards Europe, and the Community should, if possible, try and encourage the former under the guise of the latter. Associated status might be permitted, as it has been in Greece and Turkey, without a democratic procedure, but only as a preliminary encouragement towards democracy.

Such a counsel of realism may be more difficult whilst General Franco is head of state. But his long reign must surely soon end. Afterwards, the regime will be a little more shaky, at the very least, and association with an open, democratic and politically evolving Community can surely point to only one conclusion. It should be remembered that, while Spain has much to gain from the Community, she has also much to offer: Spanish labour is already well-known and liked, all over northern Europe and including Britain. Over a million

Spaniards work abroad, in Western Europe. These should be able to receive full rights as citizens of the Community, instead of the rather inferior status they have to put up with at the moment. Spain itself is already well-known to millions of northern Europeans for its incomparable holiday places. Its full integration into European society within the next generation will be most exhilarating.

Greece presents another interesting problem. Greek association occurred in 1961. Following the colonels' *coup* of 1967, the agreement was 'frozen'. Even so, there has been progress towards a customs union, but the essential accompanying measures on harmonization have not occurred, and no financial aid has been forthcoming from the European Investment Bank. In the Fifth Report of the European Communities in 1971, the Commission explicitly states that 'freezing' would continue because 'martial law continues to be in force in the regions of Athens and Salonica', comprising one-third of the population, because 'progress towards the establishment of free institutions which will ensure the return to democratic life seems to be non-existent, and because the lack of an elected Greek parliament makes impossible the proper functioning of the mixed Greek-EEC Parliamentary Committee.'

It is possible that the enlargement of the Committee could help to bring about a change in the attitude of the regime if there could be concerted action by the Nine – though it is doubtful whether the present British government will want to take any enlightened action in this respect. It is unfortunately difficult to imagine that a second Wilson regime would automatically be any more helpful. Still, Dr Mansholt's outspoken comments on the most recent iniquities in Greece may help, as in so many other matters, to create a new situation, perhaps leading to the full suspension of Association and conceivably to the collapse of the regime. Senator McGovern's comments in the election campaign of 1972 were quite encouraging in this respect.

It is also possible that a common policy by the European Communities could reach a common front on the issue of

57

Rhodesia. Sanctions by Britain have proved ineffective, but sanctions by the whole Community on that (or any similar issue) might have serious consequences.

Possibilities for ultimate association or membership exist almost everywhere in the remaining non-communist countries of Western Europe. Austria, for example, has concluded a far-reaching free-trade agreement with the Community. Political association with any other country is in fact forbidden to Austria under the terms of the State Treaty (which re-established her independence in freedom in 1955), but it seems improbable that the Soviet Union will raise serious objection to this mainly economic arrangement. The Community consumes some 60 per cent of Austria's agricultural exports (usually cattle and meat), and this percentage will increase once Britain is in the Community, since Britain and the other EFTA countries were important secondary markets, particularly for such commodities as butter and powdered milk. But the Austrian farmers are critical of the arrangements, and, since they account for 18·7 per cent of the employed population, they are quite a formidable lobby. In fact, there is a strong case for association between Austria and the Community. It is much desired in Austria, and it should be one of our political desires to attempt to achieve it.

Speaking of more general questions of foreign policy, an articulate and integrated Europe is surely likely to be a stronger force for peace, including disarmament, in all its diverse shapes, than a fragmented group of small states, such as the countries of Europe would otherwise seem, in the next generation or two. Agreements on arms limitations, for example, might be much easier, and so might East-West co-operation generally. A united Western Europe could deal more effectively with the East than could a divided one. Willy Brandt made this point very well at the Hague Summit of European Heads of Government in 1969: 'Our Community must not be a new power *bloc*, but an exemplary system which can serve as an element in the forging of a well-balanced pan-European peace settlement. . .' A European Security Conference will probably take place in 1973. If so, it will have been achieved because, and not in spite, of the new movements towards unification in the West.

It is not unfair to recall that Harold Wilson used specifically this argument in 1967, before he put forward Britain's first application for entry: 'The identification of British policy with the growing political unity of the Continent' would, he said, have two important consequences: 'The endeavours on behalf of a detente between East and West could be better co-ordinated, and a Europe that had been increased by Great Britain would be able to play a bigger role in the world.'

Since the Community has, in a general sense, made possible both the movement towards integration in Europe and its increased prosperity (which has, in its turn, helped towards the arrangement of a European Security Conference), it is naturally absurd that there should be dispute, as there seems to be, between the Commission and the European foreign ministers about the agenda for this conference. Still, the Commission's policies seem less cautious than the foreign ministers' are inclined to be, particularly over economic questions, such as credit policies or trade preferences towards Eastern Europe.

The phrase previously quoted above, 'a role in the world', may need a little elaboration. Many times in recent years, statesmen such as Mr Heath or President Pompidou have spoken of 'Europe's place' as being necessary to guarantee in the world by means of increasing its power. We hear that sort of remark with scepticism: a place in the world sounds very much like a place in the sun, and that sort of desire for assertion promises even more glumly if it is supranational rather than national. It is also obvious that the Community, with or without Britain, has a 'place in the world' whether she likes it or not, since her position in world commerce is so important and indeed predominant. Even so, however, there should be ways in which a combination of advanced and experienced countries can make contributions to the common good of humanity without seeming to be either grasping, neo-colonialist or selfish, and without entering upon the sort of commitments as a *bloc* which the European countries have dropped as individual empires and which have been assumed, almost against its will, by the US. Europe can, and should, therefore, be able to assume some form of joint responsibility for the preservation of world peace and for the welfare of all nations. A remark along these lines was made by Labour's then Commonwealth Secretary in May 1967, Herbert Bowden: 'Politically,' he said, in the House of Commons on 8 May, 'it may prove to be a considerable long-term advantage for the Commonwealth as a whole that a unified Europe, including Britain, should exert a powerful influence throughout the world and an influence that, because of Britain's membership, will automatically take account of their needs and interests.'

Even so, this sort of comment should be made with some caution. In the past twenty years, political and economic integration has begun in Europe certainly, though at a time when, for the first time for generations, as it was put by Norman Hart and Ernest Wistrich in a Fabian pamphlet in 1969, 'Europe has ceased to be the spearhead for progress and the continent from which innovation, culture and the benefits of civilization have spread to the rest of the world.'

This argument can be made even stronger. It seems platidudinous to say that the two European or world wars of this century were caused by European rivalries between the European states. In some ways, too, that definition is too broad, since both these wars, though world-wide in implication, were, to begin with, wars of the Austro-Hungarian Succession, being concerned with whether the empire of the Habsburgs would fall under German or Russian sphere of influence. But it is less obvious to assert the fundamental point that such wars will be inconceivable if in the future a European federation of the sort envisaged by the European movement is ultimately achieved.

Meantime, on one other general question of foreign policy, no one would wish to deny that Eastern Europe is a part of Europe. The Slavs were in Europe before the Saxons or the Franks. Czechoslovakia particularly, and other now lost parts of the old Austro-Hungarian Empire, along with East Germany, are territories fully within the European tradition. Our design should be that, one day, they will detach themselves from subservience to Russia (at present expressed in Russia's outrageous use of the East European economies) and enter, if not the Community, at least its orbit. Perhaps, in time, Europe could be strong enough, and Russia feeble enough, to achieve this. But it would be absurd to expect much very soon, and equally foolish to delay movements towards unity in the West in the hope that something may turn up, Micawber-like, in the East: it has not happened up till now. Nor, as suggested before, can it be honestly argued that unity in the West of Europe will diminish the chances of change in the East, or increase those of war.

These countries of Eastern Europe, although close to the West, are also traditionally and ethnically attached to Russia. That comment may not be true of Hungary, but it is certainly a correct assessment of the historic interdependence of all the Slav races over the last hundred years. Eastern Europe would be wise if it were to place as its goal over the next generation less independence from Russia, or close association with the West, than a more or less united resolve to play East and West off against each other, eschewing the crusades of 1956 or 1968, for the less romantic pursuit of the possible, as singly sought by Rumania and Yugoslavia. It should be the altruistic goal of the West to assist this. Russia itself, at least in the traditions of its intelligentsia, has equal claims to be regarded as a European country: but it has so in no other way, and it has chosen nevertheless to link itself to an Asian hinterland. Conceivably, it may happen in future that Russia beyond the Urals may be lost, or may be able to articulate non-Slav, or anti-Slav, aspirations : in which case, European Russia, large as it is, might, given a democratic development which seems improbable, be able to enter into some association with the West. If this happened it would, however, risk Russian domination. The thought is best forgotten.

The relation between defence expenditures and internal problems needs to be borne in mind. Europe is in an unmilitary mood now not only because she believes, as she has believed since 1945 (rightly), that, in the last resort, she will be protected by the US; not only because she believes the likelihood of war is remote; but because her own internal problems, though considerable, are not susceptible to the use of force (an exception is Northern Ireland and perhaps Ireland as a whole). The reverse is true of Russia and East Europe, where such stability as exists at the moment is the product of military power. But, of course, that power seems to threaten Europe, even though its day-to-day effect is to control the peoples of Russia, and of East Europe.

Speaking about international affairs in a general sense, it is difficult not to feel a certain optimism, in the short term at least. Whatever the exact cause, and whether or not the nuclear deterrent has played a serious part (or indeed any part), international peace seems as strong as it ever has done since, say, 1900: the years leading to the holocaust of 1914 were, as it now seems on analysis, very edgy and unstable, as were nearly all the interwar years with the exception of the period between Locarno and the Depression. After 1945, the cold war remained potentially explosive until at least 1962, in the sense that, at any moment, a hotter war might have broken out perhaps by accident. Since then matters have been much more quiescent, with a US-USSR summit meeting taking place in apparent amity even after Nixon's blockade of the North Vietnamese ports – an act which in the fifties would have probably led to a suspension of all meetings between the two superpowers even at the UN.

Of course, there are many local disturbances, tragic enough to the places concerned; the very stability of the international structure may have made the chances of change within the Soviet Union less likely than seemed possible in the more volatile age of Khrushchev (Michel Tatu pointed out that the explanation of Krushchev's actions in 1962 was that he was gambling on several squares at the same time: he took the decision to allow the publication in Russia of Solzhenitsyn's *A Day in the Life of Ivan Denisovich* the same month as he decided to put missiles into Cuba). It is also possible that the stability of the international scene has some connection with internal instability in several states: perhaps, as the Israeli general Harkabi once put it, we must become, in the future, accustomed to guerrilla actions interrupting the even flow of our lives as often as car accidents.[19] In this respect, it is perhaps scarcely comforting to be reminded that it has been Latin America, precisely the area of the world which has had fewer international wars, in the last century, than anywhere else, which has seen more political violence, or more politically inspired criminality, than anywhere else: peace may assure plenty but it does not always assure national cohesion. But that is one more reproach, perhaps, to the old concept of the nation state.

There is one other general point on foreign policy: the question of Germany is obviously at the heart of much British feeling about the Common Market. Germany continues to be feared by many on both Left and Right. This fear is irrational, since it derives from false views about both the past and about the future. Nazism was an evil creed, which established itself in Germany primarily because of Germany's social, political and economic weakness in the years after the First World War. That weakness was the consequence of many factors, and our own vindictiveness in 1919 was one of them. If Britain had lost the First World War, it is conceivable that a form of fascism might have taken root here too.

In the nineteenth century, many mistakes were made by British politicians who supposed that France remained the main political danger on the continent long after that had ceased to be the case. A similar error is made by those who believe that German nationalism is still a danger now. The present German Chancellor, Willy Brandt, wrote a few years ago: 'The Nazis sought to Germanize Europe after their fashion. Now the task is to Europeanize Germany.' Even if we accepted the idea that Germany could still be a danger, that remark would remain the guide to the right policy. It is, of course, quite wrong to suppose that the Germans, or any other people, are especially wicked. This sounds a platitude, but some Englishmen refuse to accept it in respect of Germany. The one thing which might have led to a revival of political criminality in Germany would have been a policy of ostracism or the adoption of the curious scheme current in the 1940s for the forced de-industrialization, or pastoralization, of the country. It might also be appropriate to recall that though Germany has committed great crimes in the twentieth century she has paid enormously in consequence, in terms of loss of territories and of lives: land which had been part of Germany since the thirteenth century is now a part of Poland and even of Russia. Bismarck, it will be remembered, once declared that the Balkans were not worth the bones of a single Pomeranian grenadier; but Pomerania is now itself Polish.

This problem of Germany seems to be one for ourselves rather than for any other West European nation. The Franco-German rapprochement of the 1950s has not been followed by an Anglo-German one, since it seemed less necessary, and since the matter seemed a more complicated one, with the decline of the British Empire. It should be one of our first preoccupations, when within the EEC, to concentrate our efforts on this side of the matter. In the sisyphean task of creating over the next generation a united Community of Europe which is socially responsible, fair to the regions, and able to evolve a credible collective will when necessary, Anglo-German friendship will be essential.

The sources of instability today seem, in fact, less national than multinational: Signor Giorgio Almirante and his fascists in Italy, the revival of anarchism, the provisional wing of the IRA, or some new form of political gangsterism, half criminal and half idealistic such as characterized much of Spanish early twentieth-century history: these are the main spectres of instability which are the obverse of the multinational company (to be discussed later) which in a different way is the spectre of political irresponsibility. There is also the possibility that one of the larger European states will lapse into civil chaos: as seemed possible in 1968 in France, and as still seems possible (though improbable) in Italy in 1972. With six counties of the United Kingdom in a state of semi-civil war, it scarcely befits Paul Johnson or Clive Jenkins to be too patronizing about the state of Europe's political stability. The dangers to liberty (as opposed to order) in the 1970s and 1980s from governments are also likely to be considerable, but they too are probably not likely to be national. It seemed symptomatic that Signor Mariano Rumor, in Milan, inaugurated the first electronic police control centre, with twenty-eight television cameras rotating from hidden places in Milan's nerve centres, on the same day – 21 April 1972 – which saw in London a debate in the House of Commons on methods of governing and regulating the storage of personal and confidential information by computer banks. These facts suggest some of the problems of the future, not the recollection of any German threat of the past.

7 Defence of a New Europe

When foreign policy is discussed, the subject of defence follows quickly and, clearly, within a few years, or even months, we may be talking again of a European Defence Community.

The very mention of the words, admittedly, recall the terrible arguments of the early 1950s which so distressed the political scene at that time. But it is well to dismiss that apparent precedent, for the circumstances are different. Europe is now in a far stronger position, and such pressure as there is to create a European defence front derives today from Europe and not, as in the 1950s, primarily from the US.

The question of the relation between Europe and defence is one upon which many members of the Labour party have strong feelings. Harold Wilson, in his speech at Labour's Common Market Conference in 1971, complained that Mr Heath, has 'repeatedly made it clear that his vision is of a Europe involving a degree of defence integration [which] none of us in this Party would accept', and again he complained that Mr Heath has not 'repudiated his ... clear advocacy of a destructive European deterrent'; while Lord Carrington had said that 'it would be wrong to rule out the possibility of collaboration – i.e. nuclear collaboration – some day'. Mr Wilson went on: 'If Conservative policy at any time were to be directed towards a nuclear component in a United Europe, a United Europe which includes Germany, any hope of a constructive reconciliation between Eastern and Western Europe would disappear.' This point of view, it should be said in fairness to Mr Wilson, characterized his speech in 1967 when advocating

66

entry into the Community: he was vigorously opposed, he said, to a joint Franco-British nuclear deterrent, despite the new concentration upon Europe which the Labour government had backed in its Defence White Paper of 1966.

Several things need to be said in response to this point of view, which has since been expressed several times, by Mr Wilson and by others. First, it is not clear whether Mr Wilson was speaking against the idea of any form of European defence structure, or only against one which included nuclear weapons. A joint planning staff is one thing, a single finger on what would be, for the moment anyway, a rather insignificant nuclear button another. It is fair to assume that Harold Wilson was only opposing European nuclear defence, not European defence in general. Second, his remarks about 'constructive reconciliation' were surely rhetorical. As it happened, progress between East and West has continued, both in respect of Herr Brandt's *Ostpolitik* and of general discussion with the Soviet Union on the subject of a European Security Treaty. Indeed, the mere fact of the *Ostpolitik* proves that an open attitude to the Eastern European countries is at least as possible from within the Community, just as de Gaulle's attitude to the Third World showed that an unaligned policy was similarly possible by a resolute member of the Community – more resolute than any European country had been, if resolution is defined as a willingness to act independently of the US since 1945. Russia has, in fact, begun to treat the Community as a serious undertaking in recent months, as she usually does when a policy of allied strength is followed through. Brezhnev virtually admitted as much in a speech on 20 March 1972. At the moment, Rumania and probably soon all the Eastern European countries are plainly preparing to come to terms with the Community. Gromyko's comment that the EEC is a monster, but one born in the zoo, must be reckoned, by Russian standards, a compliment. Thirdly, the Labour party in government was responsible for a major turn in defence policy towards Europe, and still, so far as anyone knows, or so far as its attitude towards the Defence White Paper of 1972 suggests, is determinedly

European in its outlook, so far as military matters are concerned – for the first time for many generations. The only battle for which the British army is prepared is a European battle.

In fact, I do not believe that any radical person should have any doubts *per se* about the idea of a integrated European defence force, though he might have doubts firstly as to its efficiency, secondly as to the type of weapons which it should have, and whether the idea of an 'Army' of the traditional sort represents the correct approach to the problems of self-defence. On the first score, the idea of military integration down to battalion level, as envisaged in the 1950s, is impractical for the moment; even if it were realistic, would it not become the 'sludgy amalgam' that Churchill feared it would turn into in 1951? On the second matter, some policy for rationalization and common procurement within Europe is undoubtedly desirable, if only on grounds of cost. However, the matter of weapons cannot be separated from those of common operational doctrines, joint training, and relation to both European and US technology and armament industries. The position of France is immediately raised also. The mere mention of these subjects not only suggests the complexity of the question of defence, but reminds us that defence is a matter inseparable not only from questions of foreign policy but from technology and industry as well. Britain will remain the strongest naval power in Europe, and doubtless other allocations could profitably, and sensibly, be agreed.

Up to this point in the argument, neither the question of nuclear weapons, nor that of the viability of NATO, has been raised. The idea simply is that the European contingent in NATO should be integrated, and, hopefully, become more efficient and self-reliant. Joint action would make economies possible, and make for greater European influence within NATO, as well as stimulate, in many psychological ways, the growth of political unity. The Europa cap-badge might do a good deal more than is usually supposed.

Something of this sort has already occurred, and was initiated, indeed, while Denis Healey was defence minister. Thus the

European defence ministers already meet informally before NATO meetings, in the so-called Eurogroup, served by the diplomatic permanent representatives to NATO. There is as yet no secretariat, but that doubtless will soon be possible, along with a European Defence Institute, and so on, presumably developing under the inspiration of the Eurogroup. Already, admittedly, problems as to whom to invite have cropped up: the Eurogroup includes Greece, Turkey and Scandinavia, but not France, Iceland, nor Portugal. The difficulty of developing European defence within the embrace of NATO also makes for tremendous difficulties for France, which still feels the need for obduracy in these affairs in order to placate General de Gaulle's ghost: perhaps, however, that romantic mood will one day pass. In 1972, Anglo-French defence contacts, in particular in co-operation over military aircraft, seemed to be improving. British collaboration with Germany and Italy over the multi-role combat aircraft, due to be finished in 1976, is however a much more promising and larger undertaking than anything in Anglo-French relations.

The position of nuclear weapons, if any, within such a united defence force is naturally complicated. But it is a matter which ought not to be avoided. In the preface to his Godkin lectures in 1967, Mr Heath talked of joint *planning* in respect of nuclear *strategy*, even if he admitted that joint *decisions* were, for the time being, impossible. The prospect of sharing nuclear weapons may seem disagreable, but really why should it be more so with our European allies than with our American ones? Are the French, or the Germans, more unreliable than the Americans? Unreliable in what sense? More likely to go to war? Given Europe's overcrowded continent and strategically exposed position, that is an irrational thought. But are European statesmen more likely to become irrational, or to go mad, and attempt to pursue, with nuclear weapons made in England, the foreign policy goals of the Kaiser and Hitler (or Napoleon)? It is hard to believe.

Such a discussion has, however, to be placed against the background of the real facts of the last twenty years: namely, that the nuclear powers have probably contributed to the stability of the world through their possession of nuclear weapons, and that minor nuclear powers have not, so far as it seems, actually caused greater instability. It also should occur against a consideration of likely world developments, of which the most probable and considerable is the growth of the Far East as a main centre of world dispute. The problems of China and Japan are likely to dwarf those of Europe as major unsettling matters. Europe could become, in the course of the next generation, something of a military backwater, even if economically strong: thus even taking upon herself as a continent the curious role of negativity assumed by her most economically dynamic member, Western Germany, since the war. It is also possible that, as François Duchêne has put it: 'Even if federated, with a nuclear deterrent controlled by a European president, the psychological and physical vulnerability of cramped, urbanized societies to threats of nuclear attack, and the inner diversity of what would still be a politically loose agglomeration of power, would make it inconceivable for a European deterrent to be anything but self-protective. One could not, for instance, imagine its being used as an umbrella for a second Suez adventure against some aggravating oil producer if either (or, more likely, both) super-powers were opposed.' This comment should surely go some way to smother this complaint about a European defence system; particularly when Duchêne adds, 'A nuclear European federation would be conceivable only if nuclear proliferation elsewhere had gone so far as to make any addition to the club virtually banal.'[20]

All in all, too, in the future, defence questions may occupy a less central place in the argument – and in budgets – than heretofore in the twentieth century. We may see the playing down of preoccupation with defence, perhaps under the direction of a European security commission whose task should formally be that of scaling down or stabilizing levels of armaments, as much as that of establishing security. Such a disintoxication need not make for weakness were it clear that the small forces which would seem to be thereby weakened were able to be increased quickly on a scale commensurate with any risk.

Such a qualification is certainly desirable, but may seem to beg too many questions. The fact that Europe may become a military backwater as suggested depends on its present heavy arming. At any time in the last twenty years, a real battle between East and West could easily have been totally destructive. Ivor Richard sagely pointed out: 'There is, after all, nothing quite so inhibiting as the knowledge that one risks killing perhaps three hundred million people if matters get out of hand.'[21] If nuclear weapons are left out of consideration, the military balance in Europe is not easy to assess. Measurement by divisions is confusing, since they are units larger in the West than in the Warsaw Pact. A better reckoning is troops directly available. Here, about 1·1 million of the West face about 1·3 million of the East as combat and direct forces immediately available. NATO has in fact more men theoretically under arms than the Warsaw Pact (3·4 million against 2·8 million). NATO has an inferiority in tanks of about two to one, and a less substantial one in respect of aircraft: even so, this is qualified by the NATO investment in anti-tank weapons and the high proportion of NATO's 'multirole aircraft', as it is by what must be a definite uncertainty how reliable some of the Warsaw Pact armies (Czechoslovakia and Hungary, in particular) would be in practice. Russia has also a million troops on her Chinese border. The NATO and Warsaw Pact navies break down rather evenly, with Russian superiority in submarines balanced by a Western superiority in anti-submarine craft. Still, it is the size (and character) of these forces which has helped the peace.

Realistic politics must assume that these two alliances will remain much as they are today in Europe and indefinitely so, except in consequence of agreed force reductions or changes of emphasis within the weapon systems. If this assumption is correct, then the development of a European nuclear weapon would in present circumstances be a mistake, though for reasons of cost and calculation as much as for moral reasons. The expense of a really independent weapon, with the delivery system necessary, would be great. The chances of Europe's surviving, in any reasonable way, a full nuclear war, are negligible, much more would be so in Russia or the USA, even if it were able to inflict great damage on Russia. Advanced Russian anti-missile missiles would make an effective delivery system exceptionally complicated. For the time being, and indeed for the forseeable future, the US contribution to the NATO alliance, so far as nuclear weapons are concerned, is likely to be as effective as necessary. The most astute policy for Europe, therefore, would be to make a statement in the manner of Canada that she is not going to embark upon the manufacture of nuclear weapons as a part of her system of defence. This would certainly help her general international position, and would not create any risk for the time being. A Europe, on the contrary, which is capable of standing on its own feet, so far as conventional defence is concerned, would definitely be regarded much more considerably by the USA (and probably by Russia) than one where two countries (Britain and France) are preoccupied by minor nuclear weapons which cannot be delivered.

The case for maintaining the British and the French nuclear deterrent in these circumstances needs to be re-examined carefully. (It is by no means certain that the next French governments will be so firmly convinced of the need for a deterrent as the present one; so this is not a wholly fanciful argument.) On the whole, the balance seems to be in favour of their maintenance for the time being at least ('in trust' as Mr Heath puts it, rather strongly), since it is probably desirable for Europeans to have some knowledge of, and continuing experience of, this technology, for residual military use if the US alliance were to break down. By that time too, if it occurred, presumably the MacMahon Act would also have been abrogated and, therefore, Britain would no longer be in a position to gain US nuclear information for military purposes.

The possibility of a combined nuclear deterrent with France has been much discussed, but the arguments do not seem strong. Nor, in practical terms, is it at all clear how the combination would be effected. Collaboration, in Concorde style, might be technologically possible, but what would the military effects be? Would there not be very bad blood consequently with the Germans and other Europeans?

If, however, a situation were to arise in which the USA either wished to withdraw from her commitment to NATO or seemed liable to be rendering her deterrent incredible (by neglect or preoccupation elsewhere), then a new situation would obviously arise. That has to be faced. It also has to be faced that this is a possibility over the next ten years as, indeed, France has supposed. On the whole, the expense of a European nuclear weapon system, with means of delivery, might even then be a mistake, for the reasons which make it so at the moment, but that decision might perhaps go the other way, depending on circumstances. Three points might be made: first, the degree of nuclear knowledge already possessed by the countries of Europe, and the technological knowledge in support of it, gives to Britain a permanent residual or hidden deterrent. If Russia were to threaten war on Finland, whose scientists and industry have never known how to make nuclear weapons, it would be one thing; if she were to threaten Western Europe, it would always be another, even taking into account the split-second decision-making held to be typical of the nuclear era.

The second point is that Europe derives both disadvantages and advantages from her geographical position. If we are to assume that the most probable external and direct threat to her security is Russia – a reasonable enough assumption – the manner of riposte to that country by nuclear weapons would in one way be much easier than it would be, say, to a Middle East enemy: even allowing for the 'buffer states' of the satellites, the Russian border is only five hundred miles from much of West Germany and of Italy. That makes easier the problem of a delivery; and credibility is, of course, one of the main preoccupations in consideration of the whole deterrent system. A nuclear weapon might be delivered by Western Europe against the Warsaw Pact countries by train. That could have consequences for the Warsaw Pact's conventional stance.

Thirdly, it could very well be held that the development of a

European deterrent would be against the spirit, if not the letter, of the treaty against nuclear proliferation. It might be held that, since the Germans were presumably a party to it, it would be also a breach of the Brussels Treaty by which the West Germans have given up the right to the manufacture of nuclear weapons on their own soil. Finally, it would be a bad example to the rest of the world, and probably create much dissension in Europe. The development should therefore only be considered in the extreme circumstances described above of a total US withdrawal.

Perhaps, it is as well to make one general point about our long-term attitude to foreign affairs and defence : no one, for example, believes that a sudden Russian attack on Western Europe is likely, but no one should think that such an attack, or a campaign of intimidation which might amount to the same thing, would be impossible, or even improbable, if Western Europe were defenceless. The tradition of Russian foreign policy, under the Tsars as under the Communists, has been to absorb or dominate weaker territories which are attached to it by land. This is not a revolutionary policy, concerned with the spread of communism: it is an instinctive and traditional one, concerned with the spread of Russian influence. It is one which, furthermore, characterizes most strong and powerful states, whether they are big or small. Cuba would do the same, if it could. The compulsion to organize, therefore, is strong, and in defence terms, this must mean for Europe, central power, rationalization, a common policy of arms procurement and an effective alliance structure. There is also the possibility of irrational government in Russia. If such things were to occur at a time when US preoccupations at home or elsewhere were really serious, then there might be a need for a nuclear deterrent system in Europe. The alternative would be pressure in Germany for one, since Germany would scarcely be held back from that if the protection of the US were removed.

Thus, in the short run, realism suggests that there is no alternative to the integration, and rationalization, of European defence – preferably within the present alliance, but, perhaps, able to envisage a situation where that had collapsed; or, in the long run, perhaps, when the idea of an alliance based on a nuclear deterrent was not necessary. A collapse in the internal cohesion of the Soviet Union is, at the moment, the only serious possibility for the long-term abandonment of nuclear weapons, or of any alliance based upon the residual possibility of their use. General disarmament, under general control and agreement, is an alternative, but its remoteness makes it unfortunately improbable.

A more pressing problem might be raised by the fact that all European armies except the British are, in fact, conscript ones. Conscription would not be acceptable in Britain and, indeed, the case for a professional army in the future will surely grow. Any security force possessed by the new Europe should certainly be of that character. The size of this, as of national armies in the meantime, will presumably be affected, however, by such agreements as may be reached on the subject of troop reductions at the European Security Conference.

It has been axiomatic since the First World War that no defence system can be effective without an intelligence service. How this idea came to be elaborated, and how the comprehensible aims of counter-espionage came to be interpreted as necessitating an elaborate service (or series of services) of espionage, is not quite clear. Nor is it clear how far these services, particularly since their expansion since the Second World War, have been worth the money that has been spent upon them. They have caused scandal, given material for romance or counter-romance, but it is doubtful if they have done more. A European defence service must keep its 'intelligence' side to the bare minimum and, whatever is created, keep to the rule evolved by Lord Wigg: that it must be supervized by democratically responsible leaders. (It is true, no doubt, that, when it comes to the point, European unity will only really be achieved when existing intelligence services bring themselves to be subordinate to European security; and when loyalties are so established that there can be no thought of prior confidences with other groups; even with the US.)

This may seem premature, but at least this last point is of more than usual importance because of the unpleasant role that secret services can play in the internal politics of countries particularly when these are under stress. Fortunately or accidentally, Britain has not been in this position in the last few generations, but Germany, France and Italy have, and the activities of the services of both the last two have been too near to causing civil war to be at all comfortable. It is doubtful whether we have heard the last of the Italian service of this sort. Similarly, it is obvious that even in postwar Germany, General Gehlen's organization did its best to sabotage the Social Democrats and their *Ostpolitik*. The CIA has also a number of dubious political initiatives to its discredit.

8 Europe and the Third World

It is frequently represented that the Common Market, and Britain's adherence to it, is likely to be damaging to the interests of the underdeveloped world, particularly the underdeveloped nations within the Commonwealth, but also the underdeveloped world as a whole. This is an argument which touches a raw spot among most radical people. There are very many poor people in the Third World, more and more poor people, even, who have not partaken of the increase in prosperity which has characterized the West over the last generation. Indeed, our relation with the Third World should really be a major preoccupation. The expanded Economic Community will, of course, be by far the largest market for exports from the less developed world and, doubtless, will be the largest donor of aid.

It is easy to approach this subject in an extreme fashion: 'while Europeans are calculating whether the Community can offer them a better washing machine, or more exciting holidays, a colour television, the average Third World citizen would like to see his annual income rise to above £40, to live to be older than forty-five, to be served by more than one doctor for fifty thousand inhabitants, to see fewer of his children die in infancy.' Thus, John Hatch in speaking of the discrepancy of moral values as he sees it.[22]

There is, however, an argument about what is the best way to assist these countries, and peoples. Though the EEC may seem, to the outsider, to be a kind of rich man's club, in fact, the richer the advanced countries become, the more, logically, they should be able to devote to the poor, providing they have both a conscience and the means to do it. If there are great inequalities within the advanced countries (and indeed some such remain), there will be little pressure of opinion to assist the rest of the world. The reverse is also true, as is suggested by the contributions made by the countries of the Community in contrast to Britain, over the last ten years: German trade with the Commonwealth increased 140 per cent between 1964 and 1970, while that of Britain only increased 25 per cent. Mr Ray Grantham, of the Clerical and Administrative Workers Union, put this graphically at Labour's Common Market Conference: 'Keep us out of the EEC for another ten years, and not only will we be the poorest nation in Europe, but we will be short on trade with the Commonwealth. In fifteen years' time, the value of Commonwealth preferences to us will become derisory.' Indeed, even if we were not to enter the Community, one Commonwealth country after another would make, in all probability, its own trading arrangements with the Community, as Tanzania, Uganda and Kenya did when they entered into association with the Community under the Arisha Agreement of 1968–9, and as other Commonwealth countries have done under specific trade agreements. These include Mauritius, whose main interest must be the $5M which she will receive from the European Development Fund.

Oh, well, say the anti-Marketeers, trade is not aid. What *is* aid, then? Investment? But we are at the moment less able to give aid than we might be, since we have been economically weak for so long. But as part of the Community, we could probably be more benevolent. Would not the continentals insist on helping their friends in the underdeveloped world rather than ours? To this, it can be answered that, though we have a greater knowledge of, say, India or Ghana than of French Sahara or Gabon, the differences between France and Britain over spheres of ex-imperial influence are likely to diminish. Germany and Italy, with less explicit relations with the Arab world than either the French or the British, have had already much to offer it; just as, for political reasons, Europe may have more to contribute to the countries of South America than the

USA, who knows, and is known by, those nations only too well.

It should also be evident that many underdeveloped countries have more to gain from making common cause with each other, regardless of their imperial pasts, than they have with their old European masters. The sugar problems, for example, of the Caribbean countries may be more easily considered in the light of their joint interests, than by an old piecemeal approach. The Common Market's Yaoundé Convention, with eighteen assorted African states and Madagascar, has a good deal of promise from this point of view. From the very beginning of the EEC, thanks to the French and against the wishes of the Germans, several non-European countries were brought into association with the Market; and now twenty new Commonwealth 'associables', in Africa, the West Indies and the Indian Ocean, have the chance to make new arrangements – either comprehensive trade arrangements or arrangements affecting a few items only.

The Yaoundé Convention has been criticized because of its system of so-called reverse preferences: by this, Africans offer tariff preferences to the Six on their industrial exports. The US have in particular attacked this arrangement as 'discriminatory'. Roy Jenkins, in a speech at Musselburgh, in May 1972, criticized Yaoundé, at least obliquely, by arguing that 'other African countries [must] receive equality of treatment with Yaoundé countries, and that Asian countries must also receive much freer access for their exports'. In particular, this applied to manufactured exports such as textiles and processed foods. This may seem perfectly acceptable, with the one, but major, proviso that, as even Arnold Smith, the Secretary General of the Commonwealth Secretariat, and a vigorous critic of Yaoundé, has suggested, when and after the Commonwealth has joined in, a *bloc* of thirty-eight countries will be much more influential than one of eighteen.

As to the outright aid, the plain truth is that nearly every member of the Community contributes more per head to the underdeveloped world than Britain does at the moment; and a recent survey has suggested that, while most continental Europeans were anxious to help people overseas, over 50 per cent of those asked in Britain were uninterested. Such evidence as exists also suggests that opinion in the EEC of the Six is at least as interested in the rest of the world as is Britain, which has sometimes seemed to have been going through a rather introspective stage. British adherence to the Community will also probably make it easier for us to draw towards the target for aid to underdeveloped countries of 1 per cent of GNP, as suggested by the Pearson Report in the UN : of which 0·7 per cent was to be official aid, and 0·3 per cent private aid, in the form of loans, investment and so on. The European Commission in February 1972 called for a commitment to the 1 per cent target by 1975 (in 1970, Belgium, France and the Netherlands reached their 1 per cent target; Germany and Italy fell below it, though they had reached it in 1969; the Netherlands contributed 1·41 per cent), stressed the need for grants not loans, and adopted a progressive comprehensive trade and aid approach – even suggesting that the Community might adhere to the International Sugar Agreement. Mr Pierre Harmel of Belgium has proposed a Marshall Aid plan for the Third World. West Germany's very positive attitude at the UNCTAD Conference in Santiago in 1972 might be compared with the rather discouraging one of Britain. In subsequent months, spokesmen for the Community have made imaginative proposals to help other parts of the world, including a £15M plan for Palestinian refugees (the leakage of which scheme much irritated Sir Alec Douglas-Home) and a scheme for industrial advice to the Andean group of countries.

Admittedly, these things are not as straightforward as they seem. In many ways, France, the leader in proposing the Yaoundé Convention, has simply carved out for herself a new economic empire in Africa, with none of the expenses of direct rule. Thus the Ivory Coast is supposed to be a model for French and European relations with the Third World; but, in practice, the commerce and industry is largely in French hands, and there is little restriction of repatriation of profits to France. French personnel has multiplied much since independence, unemployment has apparently continued or even increased, and the value of imports, not exports, has gone up. The European Development Fund has not done much, either, to prevent this situation occurring elsewhere. This is an area where British adherence to the Community could help a good deal. It will certainly not do so if it stays outside. (This is not confined to France: Russia has been recently receiving more in debt repayment than she has paid out.)

In the next few years the old concept of aid, in the form of cash loans or grants for specific undertakings, will probably disappear, being replaced by agreements whereby advanced countries try and arrange not to produce, for perhaps strategic or traditional reasons, crops which can more cheaply be produced abroad. The best example of what might be done can be seen in respect of sugar, the main product of a number of tropical countries, in the form of cane, and one where the advanced countries compete, in the form of beet. But a pound of sugar made from beet costs two and half times what it would cost if made from cane, transport costs taken into account. The sugar made from each of them is the same in consistency. Why, then, do the European, Russian, and Mid-West farmers produce such quantities of sugar themselves? Because the beet farmers of these countries have constituted a powerful interest group, and because governments fear that they will be cut off from tropical sugar supplies during wars. But, if the advanced countries really wished to help the Caribbean and other tropical sugar producers, they would try and scale down gradually their consumption of sugar from home sources and increase that which comes from abroad. The enlarged EEC will be in a strong position to use its influence on behalf of the Third World and, perhaps, to suggest the kind of world division of labour that this scheme would demand.

It is also obvious that similar arrangements might be proposed in respect of the oil producing countries of the Middle East, and of many less technically demanding manufactures, such as suits, shoes, furniture, chemicals, all of which can be made cheaply in the Third World and not less expertly. Since the war, nearly half the textile workers of Britain have been redeployed in other industries, leaving about 40 per cent of our textiles to be supplied by the Third World. This arrangement and these percentages could, given the right leadership, be made mandatory throughout the continent.

The attraction of arranging aid through Europe is that it makes possible common, multilateral aid, under the European Development Fund, which would replace bilateral aid, which often has severe strings attached (special rights, loans etc.) and frequently has neo-colonialist overtones. Bilateral aid also maintains the division of the developing countries, especially Africa, into spheres of interest. Of course, the underdeveloped world is not a monolithic gathering, nor is it a static one. Brazil and Cuba, Burma and South Korea, have different political systems and pasts, different growth rates and different problems. Haiti's GNP per head is $80 a year, Venezuela's nearly $1,000; Chad and Libya have similar differences. The critical question is one of leadership and decision-making, as well as one of need. Brazil, the most aggressive country of the underdeveloped world, seems liable to make a bid for its leadership.

In 1962, the Labour Party's National Executive stated firmly, 'If, by joining the Common Market, we could mobilize the economic resources of Europe to help the underdeveloped nations of the world, and to promote the cause of world peace, by ensuring more creative and liberal policies in Europe, then the case would indeed be strong'.[23] The case is strong indeed from that point of view, as it is from the angle of political realities ten years later.

A recent idea for a new approach to effective aid was the proposal discussed at the UNCTAD conference in Santiago, whereby the underdeveloped world would receive special drawing rights created by the IMF and distributed among its member countries in proportion to planned quotas – each developed country foregoing a portion of its allocation in proportion to its GNP. The amounts foregone would be given to multilateral aid agencies for distribution.

Another important point is that multilateral aid, under the aegis of the Community, would be more likely to be nonpolitical and non-ideological in character, without too great reliance on zones of influence. It stands to reason that arrangements for the linking of aid and conservation are much more likely to be worked out in the style necessary: 'Both inequality between nations and conservation are world problems if they are agreed to be problems at all,' wrote Ian Little, 'and the same is true of some pollution. Measures which contributed to these three problems (which have world-wide application) would be an expression of world solidarity, which is more appealing, and might be more effective, than the two world concept promoted by UNCTAD.'[24]

Europe's power to help will increase, too, in inverse proportion to the extent that it seems a future master. This is one of François Duchêne's many incisive points in his recent essay 'Europe's role in world peace'. Pointing out that, to both East and South, 'the route is blocked', he rightly concludes that Europe may have a 'functional sphere of interest, but it is most unlikely to have a geographical one'. He also urges that the European countries should avoid at all costs what might be described as an 'exemplarist' heresy. Even if Europe were to achieve a model society, tolerance and order embracing, along with other unlikely couples (bureaucracy and participation, centralism and regionalism), it could not really be a model as such for countries of the Third World, the conditions of whose political history are so different. Tolerance, liberty, community interests, the absence of glaring contrasts may be absolutes, where they are satisfactorily defined: in particular, it might be said, tolerance to political exiles – an old role of Britain and France, at least. But the history of Europe does not prove the method exactly to achieve them elsewhere. On the other hand, a creative European federation in which central and regional powers were properly balanced might very well have attractions in other continents once they had approached our levels of economic achievement.

9 Europe, the UN and World Prospects

Radical people in this country have been used, in the fifty years since 1919, to look at the nation state with a jaundiced eye, and to believe that, in the long run, the only hope for humanity was some form of world union. Hence, the active backing and enthusiasm by many for the League of Nations, for the cause of world disarmament and, to a lesser extent, for the UN. In the 1950s, there were enthusiasts for disarmament who looked at that project as being likely to create the outline for a world organization. In the last few years, enthusiasm both for disarmament as for world unity has diminished. The reasons are the same: a reluctance to accept any existing world order based on the present balance of forces. Any world state created now, for example, would give undue importance, as many would say, to the USA; and disarmament might limit the possibilities of wars of liberation. Thus it is difficult to know who likes the idea *tout court* of a world state: the Left certainly do not want it, now, and the Right have never done more than pay lip service to it.

Still, the probability is that this ideal is more likely to be realized, if ever, through the type of gradual development characteristic of the European Market than by any other means. Hugh Gaitskell spoke of this in a speech at a meeting of the World Parliamentary Association in Paris in October 1962, and said that he believed a united Europe could be a 'building block for world government'. Whether indeed the blocks do lead to world government is a different matter. At the moment, *faute de mieux*, it would seem more probable that we shall move

towards a world of *blocs tout court*. A recent editorial in the
Fabian international journal *Venture* puts the subject in an
Orwellian manner: 'even now, one is beginning to discern the
shadows of a new grouping of the world, in which the US,
Europe, Russia and China face each other, the US with Latin
America for a dependency, Europe with Africa for a dependency, China fighting for supremacy in South Asia, and Russia
uncertain whether to compete against China or throw in her lot
with Western Europe. It is not a scene in which one can see
much place for world government.'[25] One need not necessarily
accept this prophecy to see that it is a more probable one than a
quite new, and presumably partially centralized, world state.

At the same time, many of the arguments about sovereignty
and nationalism are put forward from a very narrow historical
point of view. There is admittedly no doubt that the most important political occurrence of the last few generations has been
the development of the nation state. This has naturally trans-
formed, in all countries, all discussion of the role of the
individual, and his relation with authority and with society. It is
fair to point out, however, that it has been a very recent
development and that on the whole it caused more misery than
happiness. Its recentness can be most easily grasped by
considering that at the time of the birth of both my own
grandfathers, in the 1850s, neither Italy nor Germany were
united, nor did central Europe or Russia boast anything like
the governments which have since been created in their territories. Only Britain, the Netherlands and France, and Spain
and the USA to a lesser extent, had the sort of national undertaking which we now assume to be inevitable. Outside these
areas, class and tribe were the dominant divisions in society.
The on the whole malevolent course of history which our communities have politically followed since 1850 is obviously most
clearly expressed in the two world wars, in the effort to create a
similar state in Russia under Stalin and in the gradual assumption of Europe's bad example by the rest of the world. The fact
that this represents the history of the last hundred years should
not, however, make us think it was in any way inevitable.

There were many in nineteenth-century Germany and Italy, as in the Habsburg empire, who deplored the course of events which liberal fashion, and the strong desire to emulate Great Britain and France, seemed to dictate. Afterwards, hostility to the state passed from the hands of romantic Neapolitans to a socialist proletariat, many of whose leaders, however, being middle class in origin, were soon persuaded that they could, in a limited way, use these modern states for benevolent purposes. On the whole, they were wrong. They were also wrong in believing Marx, and Lenin, when they argued that capitalism inevitably led to war. It was, in fact, nationalism, undertaken in defiance of material considerations, that inspired the wars.

The new nation states of the Third World, incidentally, are fundamentally different from those of the old world since they have little control over their own political and economic problems. But they, too, have usually made political or idealistic rather than material or economic choices.

This does not lead to an argument for a world state. Indeed, little could be more gloomy a prospect in present circumstances. A single authority, centrally directed, would probably have to resort to barbarism to ensure anything like efficiency. The chances of such a state adopting civilized standards are remote. Far more important is the possibility of securing some means of ensuring the continued, or even greater, diversity of existing societies by means of lowering to more local levels many political decisions, disintoxicating national political life without, however, losing social control. This is afforded significantly by the way the European Community may perhaps develop, given decision, imagination and courage in the next few years.

Part II

1 Change in Society

One change which seems imminent in consequence of joining the Community is the proposal that British barristers should adapt their professional practices to continental methods: towards, for example, making it possible for clients to consult barristers directly, without going through solicitors, and even for solicitors to plead in courts. This amalgamation of the two branches of the legal profession has been for generations discussed in England without anything happening, along with other new ideas. Now the possibility of merging British with European legal practices, long overdue as most would say, seems closer – much closer than, as it has turned out, it was in 1964, when a Labour government was elected on the promise of these, and other, legal reforms.

This change, important in itself, is symptomatic of many which will become possibilities after Britain is fully within the Community. Everywhere the ice is breaking, no one quite knows where the water will flow but, obviously, within Europe, society will be on the move, for good or evil. Here is a great chance to secure that these changes of attitude, of custom, and of institution, are generously, creatively, and wisely effected.

Obviously, no sane person believes in change for its own sake: in some respects, indeed, we should be prepared to recognize, as the late John Strachey cleverly foresaw might be the case as long ago as 1950, that Conservatism might become a party of nervous, irrational change, and Labour, one of consolidation, even, on occasion, of conservatism. Europe, however, offers many attractive possibilities for those prepared to be optimistic about the desirability of structural change.

Britain and Europe of the Six approach many social problems from different postures. The continental background of Roman law, on the one hand, clashes with the English tradition, giving, among other things, a quite different role to police and judiciary in criminal cases; the enquiry before a case being made on the continent by the magistrate, and not by the police. Who is to say that the first plan has nothing to commend it here? The position of the Church of Rome in the countries of the Six gives them, at the least, a different cultural tradition, and precisely a different spring to all parties of the Left, which began as, and to some extent remain, anticlerical – that in itself being, in part, the explanation of the greater role played by Marxism in their formulation: a strong Church can only be displaced by a prophet. The differences are also striking in terms of education and attitudes to the family. If Europe makes further steps towards unity, it will be essential to see that these diversities profit each other, rather than the reverse: the first is possible, and so is the latter.

It is perfectly natural to speak of European social policies, and the collaboration of cross fertilization between them, as if it were a branch of technology : more sharing of information, less duplication of research, more resources for joint undertakings and so on. There are, however, evident limits. The sharing of information is one thing, but, as yet, there is in Europe no uniformity, or breath of it, about, for example, the training of doctors, or diagnosis. Even in England, no one agrees whether hospitals should be large or small, how to decide who precisely should receive help from a kidney machine, how much money to spend on the screening of possible future diseases by, for example, cervical smears, or by chest X-rays. There are similar uncertainties about priorities in all respects of the other main social services, such as housing and welfare, generally, not to speak of education. Is it enough to say that entry into the Community will affect this if it is followed by the gradual or swift establishment of a European department of social security? Of course not. The only immediate effects in this field of joining the Community will be that continental regulations on social security for migrant workers will take the place of the bilateral agreements Britain has already concluded with the Six; and members of the healing professions will have freedom to practice in any part of the Community.

There is, of course, no truth in the wild suggestion that the British Health Service will be abolished; nor, indeed, that that service is so superior to continental practice as by itself to encourage a flood of 'foreign' labour – as is sometimes suggested might be the case. In all social matters, Britain differs so substantially from the countries of the continent that the immediate consequences of entry will be slight to begin with, and will only start to have an effect after some years, and then perhaps indirectly: our houses will remain indefinitely with a far higher percentage of owner-occupied (but continental methods of housing finance may be introduced), our education divided between private and public. For the forseeable future, this subject should remain a matter for persuasion, influence, and interchange of ideas: with, in the long run, joint policies over special problems (treatment of the mentally ill, for example) being allowed to take priority.

Education within the European Community remains as yet untouched by the new institutions. Systems of schools and universities, nationally constructed at the time of the rise of literacy in the early part of this or the nineteenth century, continue strong national biases, in curricula and organization. True, there is the plan for a European university, and some other multinational projects. But, in the beginning, our membership of the EEC will have no direct effect upon education. After all, even in countries with autonomous regions, education is one of those matters where decisions are best devolved. On the other hand, it is clear that if the politicians and the leaders of opinion of tomorrow are to think or behave in a way that Europe, rather than their old national loyalties, takes precedence, then the education systems of to-day will have to be inspired consciously with the ideals of European integration. Decisions in adult life, particularly decisions at moments of crisis, always reflect the outlook of education. In enquiring into the motives of those who took the fatal decisions in 1914, James Joll rightly pointed out, in his inaugural lecture on becoming Stevenson Professor of International Relations (entitled '1914, The Unspoken Assumptions'), that we could do worse than investigate the school curricula of the 1870s.

Several other things at least demand mention. Continental countries are experiencing a crisis in their educational systems. So are we, in a less obvious way. The crises are similar, even though the causes are different. Graduates are increasing, standards at universities are under pressure (on the continent collapsing), schoolchildren question the moral authority of school teachers. Education has become an obsession of parents, a substitute for religion and even for all moral direction whatever; but there are many quite fundamental doubts as to what education is. In all European countries, social status before school age determines much, even within the public section of education. The relation between education and life, or vocation, is undefined, and that is often a reflection of the undefined relation between school and locality. The institution of the school seems almost as menacing in large modern schools in cities as it was in the old monastic public school of Dr Arnold or Talbot Baines Reed. Can education be seriously improved without serious changes in the social structure?

The probability is that our entry into Europe will begin to influence education sooner than we suppose. The increasingly internationally minded students of the present will demand common holiday times, perhaps, and from that will be one step towards the discussion of common syllabuses. Several preliminary steps along these lines should be taken as soon as possible : and it might lead to many political dividends if we were to accept, and press for the acceptance by others, of the old idea that French might become the universal second language, at first in Europe and then in the world. The achievement of such a reform, leading to the possibility of real international comprehension in an obvious way as well as satisfying the latent French linguistic chauvinism, might be one of the main benefits of a European education structure.

Two questions stand out from this analysis: they relate to race and to women.

Fair shares for black or Indian people is a matter where, for obvious social and historical reasons, the same criteria do not apply on the continent as they do in England. Commonwealth immigrants who become British citizens will be able to seek and accept employment in the European Community; but this right will presumably not apply to Commonwealth immigrants who are not citizens of the UK. (Nor will temporary immigrants to, say, Germany from Turkey or Greece be able to come to Britain.) But private and public authorities can practise an infinite variety of prejudices. The Dutch police, for example, are known to have an admirable record on racial questions, the French less so. Some form of European undertaking on racial matters would evidently be desirable. On the whole, racism on the continent has been quiet since 1945, and no French election or political party has been disturbed by racial questions in the same way as the British have been. But the French have certainly seen the development of Bidonvilles of Algerian workers in the suburbs of Paris, whose conditions are as bad as some of the ghetto-like communities of Pakistanis or Indians in Wolverhampton or Bradford.

On the whole, there is no reason at all to suppose that colour questions will be adversely affected by British adherence to the European Community, and the effects may, on the contrary, be very beneficial. This is likely particularly in Mediterranean areas, which are traditionally far less stuffy on racial questions than are the Anglo-Saxons.

As for women, the Treaty of Rome (Article 119) called for equal pay between the sexes for equal work. Though this has not been achieved, the 22 per cent of women who are in employment at all earned three-quarters of what men did in the old EEC, compared to about one half in Britain (the countries of the European Community, like Britain, have a small numerical superiority in favour of women, with the preponderence of women over men specially marked, for obvious historical reasons, in Germany). Female earnings have apparently grown at a faster rate than those of male workers in the Community, so that the gap between male and female earnings is growing narrower on the continent than it is here. This is partly because of the jobs they do in the two areas, but not entirely. Still, women on the Continent remain 20 per cent less well off than their male colleagues, while skilled ones are 35 per cent less well off. Various problems, common to all Europe, seem to threaten women's general position: thus certain sectors of industry – such as the clothing, shoe and food trade – are certain to be overhauled, reducing the number of jobs. Newer, more technical jobs may go to men, even if office jobs will probably go to women. Women, therefore, should seek to secure even entry into all jobs and professions, and they should be prepared to establish separate branches within unions to secure this.

Patterns of female employment obviously differ. Forty-seven per cent of the female population of France have a job, but only 26 per cent in Holland. In France one-third of women workers are in agriculture, 52 per cent in Germany and less than 10 per cent in Holland and Britain. This last percentage is, however, rapidly dwindling since many are old, or over forty, looking after uneconomic smallholdings. In most European countries, women dominate primary and pre-school education, and make an important contribution to secondary education. But many women work, unpaid, in family shops or farms. These differences make it difficult to suggest a common policy. Perhaps such a thing is far from a priority. But women in general should look towards European membership quite enthusiastically from the point of view of wages. Common policies are provided for, and they are likely to be influenced by existing practice in the continental societies.

2 Social Security and Labour

The British Trade Union movement will, from 1 January 1973, be the largest single European movement of organized labour, just as the Confederation of British Industries will be the strongest national industrial pressure group within the Community. The Confederation of Shipbuilding and Engineering Unions will be the biggest industry-wide negotiating organization. In comparison, continental unions are politically divided (and, except in Germany, divided on religious grounds), and no industrial group has the same organizing power as the TUC. British trade unions are also the oldest established. Still the Second World War and the Nazi or fascist dictatorships destroyed most continental unions, and 1945 gave an opportunity for reconstruction on a new rational basis: and, so far as trade union organization is concerned, at least, it is obvious that Nietzsche was right and that a great victory is worse than a great defeat. Many people in English industry must envy Germany their famous rationally based eighteen unions reorganized after 1945, partly on the recommendation of Vic Feather.

There are many other important differences too in the practice of continental unions with, for example, there being no equivalent to the British 'closed shop'. Plant bargaining is rare.

The strength of the British trade unions does not by itself mean that our practices are likely to be adopted all over the continent. On the contrary, there are several ways in which it is probable that, over the next few years, British, rather than continental, ways will change. Thus, continental workers, at the moment, take more account of conditions of work, of holidays, confinement payments, and other such 'fringe benefits' in their collective agreements. On the other hand, methods of comparison between conditions of employment and even earnings are surprisingly difficult, even in these advanced countries such as we all are, since the criteria are different in such statistics as exist. The harmonization of statistics should be one of the early tasks for the European Statistical Office after 1973. Therefore what can now be said is much less complete than it should be. It can nevertheless be said explicitly that already, in the Six, it is more difficult to dismiss workers than in Britain, though there are differences in treatment. Employees can be dismissed everywhere for 'serious offences', but in all the Six save for France and Belgium, companies have to provide a series of motives before giving notice to labour. In both Germany and Italy, contracts can be broken verbally, but in Italy workers can demand written explanations from employers. In all states of the Community, workers' councils have to be consulted before action occurs.

It also seems clear that, all the time during the 1960s, real wages have gone up in the Community faster than they have in Britain, along with pensions, benefits, and holidays: so much faster, indeed, that, in the twelve years since the formation of the Community, Britain's average wage has been outstripped by all the European countries. A recent estimate is that average British wages are $2799 a year, and wages in the European Community $3566. The standard of living, reckoned by the usual criteria, is higher on the continent than it is here, taking into account items like wages, hours of work, social benefits, paid holidays etc. These materialist arguments were first put by those within the Labour movement and others who favoured the EEC in 1961 or 1962. The anti-Marketeers replied that a better solution to the problem thus suggested was a Labour government. That expedient was ultimately applied. But, after six years of a Labour government, the statistics suggested that Britain was by then at the bottom of the European table for real wages and for benefits (having been at mid-point in 1958), while unemployment had risen to become a major social problem for the first time since the war.

TRENDS IN WAGES AND LIVING COSTS

	Consumer Price Index 1970 [100 = 1958]	Hourly gross Wage Index 1970 [100 = 1958]	Real Rise in Wages since 1958	Wages (in $ per employed person) 1958	1969
Belgium	131	214	56%	1846	3811
France	164	252	54%	1730	4176
Germany	133	259	95%	1461	3470
Italy	148	284	92%	1033	2812
Luxembourg	130	215	62%	2488	4037
Netherlands	159	275	73%	1432	3987
UK	151	196	30%	1677	2799
			(EEC average –	1455	3566)

Source: ECSO (European Community Statistical Office)

It has been suggested that these statistics are unsatisfactory, or are inadequately put together in some way. 'You people can do anything with figures', a music lover once exclaimed in dudgeon, when her claim that Purcell had plagiarized Handel was refuted by the rejoinder that the latter was ten when the former died in 1695. It is possible that the initial base of earnings in 1957 may have been higher in Britain than in the EEC and that, therefore, continental earnings may have been catching up with those here. Such figures also usually exclude the self-employed and any unearned income. An index of hourly earnings in manufacturing industries alone puts British earnings fourth out of seven in Europe, above Germany: so that other sectors in the British economy (such as services in the nationalized industries) have obviously been lower. In certain areas, such as Coventry, wages in the engineering industry exceed national averages on the continent. But the statistics are broadly comparable for the average working week. However, the complications grow when it is recalled first that the average working week is longer, on the whole, on the continent than

95

the forty hours normal in Britain, but, second, that the average number of hours actually worked here far exceeds the standard working week in all countries. The average hours worked by manual workers in Britain was 45·7 in October 1970 (for males: females, 37·9), whereas on the continent it was 44·1. Without troubling the reader with the labyrinthine differences which distinguish overtime payments in the different countries, it is worth appreciating that there are, on the continent, such things as 'performance supplements', and supplements which increase after the second hour or afterwards. Thus it can well be appreciated that levels of earnings give a quite wrong impression of actual incomes, particularly when, in the countries of the Community, employers pay more of the social security contributions than they do in Britain. It certainly can be said that, in the Community, wages are more close to spendable income. The overall impression, taking everything into account, is that, with few exceptions, workers in the European Community are better off reckoned in sheer financial terms than they are in Britain.

In respect of unemployment, it should perhaps be recalled that the problem, in the 1970s, is of a different sort from what it was before the war: the mass misery of unemployment, with low dole payments, lasting for many years, which was a characteristic of pre-war unemployment is mercifully not a feature of the present scene. Of course, too, the causes of modern unemployment are several, and here, the European Community cannot, obviously, offer final answers. But the Community of the Six has certainly achieved lower rates of unemployment; and it is also relevant to recall the remark, at the Labour Party Conference in 1971, of John Mackintosh, MP: 'If we had had one year of the growth which all the Common Market countries have had, we should still have been in power to-day'. (The only qualification to be made here is that the rates for real unemployment in Italy and, to a lesser extent, in France are difficult to estimate. Most people would suspect that the figures over-estimate the real unemployment figures. There are many in those countries who are registered for unemployment, but who seem actually to be in work.)

RELATIVE UNEMPLOYMENT RATES

	December 1971
UK	*969,874*
Germany	*269,800*
France	*397,900*
Italy	*1,088,900*
Netherlands	*114,500*
Belgium	*99,000*
Luxembourg	—

Source: Department of Employment, ECSO.

The history of the European Community has also shown a steady drop in unemployment in all member countries except in France – where there has been a slight rise from a low figure in 1958 of only 1 per cent of the active population to 1·7 per cent. Admittedly, there are regions, and age groups, where unemployment remains high: Southern Italy and lower Saxony, Italy and France among teenagers, Germany among over sixties. Coal mining has seen in the Community a 60 per cent decrease in numbers of jobs since 1958, and in agriculture (even before the Mansholt Plan) 40 per cent, just as the chemicals and plastics, rubber and engineering industries have expanded. A mild rise in 1972 in overall unemployment also seems to have ocurred, especially in Italy – explicable probably by political and economic uncertainty.

It is also evident that the benefits under social services are higher on the continent than they are in Britain. The proportion of national expenditure spent on social security is higher in the Community, and all the countries separately spend more per head than Britain does. Indeed, the expenditure in most of the Community (except Italy) is half as much again at least as that spent in Britain. In 1968, Britain spent 12·4 per cent of her GNP on social security, while Germany spent 16·5 per cent, France 15·9, Italy 16·5 and the Netherlands 17·5.

97

Family allowances are two to three times higher in the Community than they are in Britain, and their cost is largely met by industry. The taxpayer is therefore also better off. Social security benefits are very much higher in the countries of the Six than in England. Similarly, the continental European worker enjoys two to three times as many paid holidays as he would in this country, or in Ireland.

RATES OF UNEMPLOYMENT IN THE EUROPEAN
COMMUNITY

	1958	*1970*
Germany	*2·9*	*0·6*
France	*1·0*	*1·7*
Italy	*6·2*	*3·2*
Belgium	*3·7*	*2·2*
Netherlands	*2·5*	*1·1*
Luxembourg	*0*	*0*

These simple statements can only be made, admittedly, after an elaborate enquiry into such matters as the extent to which some countries (such as Italy) give extra holidays in considera-tion of age, and others even (such as Luxembourg) in recog-nition of youth – both ideas being examples of generosity which should be copied where possible. There are also holiday bonuses in Germany, and more public holidays.

It is possible too, that, since the Treaty of Rome insists on 'fair competition' between member states, the British method of financing their social services will alter, but the proportion of financing by the government has been growing in the Community countries. The continental method of payment means that an automatic accelerator is applied to benefits which are linked to the cost of living through earnings. This said, it should be appreciated that there is a difference in principle between continental and British social services at the moment. The British 'Beveridge' system guarantees a basic sub-sistence income, contributions being levied by a flat rate: the continental system seeks to consider not the ideal but the practical, and tries to ensure that people are provided with enough to make up for losses. The normal principle is that the benefit, and the contribution, are related to earnings. The continent, on the whole, has no health service as such: the various funds pay the doctor, or the hospital, as the case may be. There remain substantial differences in methods of payment, and application, too, within all the continental countries. On balance, it seems that the different schemes on the continent are in practice at least as generous as, and probably more so in some ways than, the British ones. For example, the age at which family allowances stop is usually higher in the Community countries, the allowance is usually paid for the first child and does not begin at the second, waiting day regulations are generally less (in respect of both health and unemployment) and so on.

SOURCE OF FINANCE OF SOCIAL SECURITY

	Employer	Employee	State
UK	20	22	58
France	69	22	9
Germany	49	31	20
Belgium	50	23	27
Italy	66	17	17
Netherlands	46	39	15
Luxembourg	40	23	37

Source: ECSO, quoted Coventry and District Employers Association, *Labour Relations and employment conditions in the EEC*, p. 103.

It is desirable to dwell on these things, since although the European Community as such is not involved by these activities of its members, it probably will become so. A European social code is a likely development within the next few years, and it will be partly anyway based on current practices. These practices, too, were embarked upon within the psychological background afforded by the Community, even if they were not created by it. The main examples of action by the Community as yet, are the provisions for free movement of labour and the agreement on working hours in agriculture.

In May 1972, the Commission called on the governments of the EEC to co-ordinate their redundancy laws. The Commission has proposed a plan whereby employers should not only give written justification for each dismissal, but six weeks' notice: in cases of collective dismissal, precise rules should also be drawn up. The Commission has added that particular consideration should be given to the age of workers concerned. The six weeks' notice might be increased as workers get older, and might be set at three months for those over forty, and six months for the over fifties. Governments should also be able to impose waiting periods in which dismissals would be suspended. The Commission added that a consideration of dismissals and redundancies should be linked to a consideration of 'continuity of employment', whereby new jobs would be rapidly found for all dismissed.

Of the existing arrangements on social security in the Community, that on movement of labour is the most far-reaching. The ban on discrimination based on nationality came into force in 1968. Since then, workers have been able to travel from state to state in order to look for work, and not only when an offer of work has been made. Such workers merely have to obtain a residence permit (issuable for five years, and renewable automatically) and are helped to find work, if they need it, by an office dependent on Brussels. Similarly, all are entitled to the rates of social security benefit in the country which they have got to. Other discriminations against migrant workers have been actively discouraged. By 1970, about one million nationals of one member country of the Community were employed in other member states. The main recipient has been Germany. The livelihoods of two million people are probably involved in this migration – mostly unskilled, mostly in Germany or France, and mostly in metal manufacture services or building (this compares with about two and a half million immigrant workers from non-Community countries, and about three hundred thousand Community nationals employed outside the Community, particularly Switzerland).[26]

It is not quite clear what the effect has been of these provisions on the movement of labour. Shortages of skilled labour, and even of labour generally, have affected the question. Statistics are astonishingly difficult to gather. Now that Britain has joined the Community, British labour will, of course, be affected, and, presumably, that will affect the unemployment situation in Britain. The provisions for free labour movement in the Treaty of Rome have undoubtedly helped to reduce the severity of unemployment in Italy. On the other hand, continental Europeans are somewhat more accustomed to migration and, therefore, maintain a positive attitude to it. Perhaps this was due to the war and to the major emigrations that followed. This was one of the factors, indeed, leading to the idea of European integration. It certainly is a stronger influence among continental Europeans than it is in Britain. A reluctance to move about may be one reason for Britain's relatively poor rate of growth. Thus, it would be foolish to think that this stipulation opens the way to a promised land in Britain. But a steady flow of British workers to Germany is likely over the next ten years.

It is worth mentioning that one of the few positive consequences of mass tourism has been the increased tolerance of foreign workers and their customs. (Tourism, as much as anything else, has had a similar tolerant effect on students.) The question of migrant labour should, of course, be partly considered in relation to regional questions too.

In May 1972, Albert Borschette, the Commissioner for competition policy, announced that the Commission proposed to make a big effort to establish uniform wage rates, working hours and labour conditions throughout Europe – 'so that differences, under this heading, between member countries shall cease to be a factor in determining where investment shall be located'. Substantial progress in this would, of course, be somewhat embarassing for the British government and for British industry. The low wage rates in Britain in comparison with the continent partly explains why British exports are competitive, despite often lower productivity. Perhaps, this statement by itself shows to what extent the issue of comparability of wages with the continent is bound to become an issue in British labour politics.

Within the Community also, it should be easier for international labour to challenge the newest capitalist innovation, the multinational company. International wage bargaining took place in 1968–9 in the international subsidiaries of the French Saint Gobain glass trust. The US car workers called, some years ago, for the establishment of a world-wide car-workers' union, though the difference between unions in Europe and in Japan, not to speak of wages, has naturally prevented anything happening for the time being. A meeting was convened in June 1972 at Geneva of car workers in Europe. Moss Evans, British liaison secretary of the group, made a speech in Hastings on 24 May 1972: it was essential, he said, that the union should have a strategy to match that of multinational organizations, who were free to move capital and whole areas of their operations across national borders. Mr Evans realized that it was difficult, to begin with anyway, to try and establish international wages, but hours, holidays and general conditions of work could be discussed. The same week that Moss Evans was explaining this doctrine, shop stewards in Milan and in Liverpool announced a one-day strike as a protest against the sackings, closures and short-time working that Dunlop-Pirelli has suffered since their merger in March 1970. The consequence was that on 9 June 1972, ten Dunlop or Pirelli factories, out of fifty-five in Britain, stopped work, and nearly all factories stopped work in Italy. One report suggested that the British and Italian collaboration in itself led to some 'eye-openers': the Italians were impressed by the British 'stint' payment system, whereby an agreed price is struck for an agreed output. The British were surprised to find how extensive Italian fringe benefits and holidays are: 'pound for pound', said Charles Parker, deputy governor of the Dunlop rubber workers, to a British newspaper correspondent, 'the Italians probably don't earn any more than we do, but they have a far better set of working agreements than we have'. Soon afterwards, a conference of European trade unions at Geneva approved the idea of a new, continent-wide trade union system, and even began to discuss a statute, secretariat and so on. All this activity occurs admittedly not at the behest of the Community, but once again within the psychological environment created by the Community.

These sentiments have more support even among British labour than is sometimes supposed. Thus, the annual conference of engineering workers in June 1972 backed a campaign to withdraw from the Community: but several strong speeches were made rejecting this attitude by, for instance, James Conway, the Union's Secretary General, who said, 'I believe in a United States of Europe, since I am a socialist. We have never examined what Europe is about. We just run away from it in fear. Yet one day our children will be talking about the fight we had in the same way as we talk about the Battle of the Roses ... we are faced with the challenge of Europe, and you cannot stand on one side and be little saints . . .' And Mr Weakley, from Swansea, said that his brand of socialism was not to build a society where only workers of Manchester united, but where workers of the world unite. It is likely that these and other similar voices will remain resonant in the future.

Since the *événements* of Paris in 1968, the word of the hour has been 'participation'. The fashion for this has been directly related by an effort by workers, students, ordinary people everywhere to secure some position of consequence within the often large and dull, though efficient, institutions in which they have their livelihood. On the continent, generally, however, a form of industrial democracy has been practised since 1945. The French profit-sharing scheme does not merit some of the attacks which have been made on it. But it is in Germany that participation has most developed, under the system of *Mitbestimmung* (co-determination). This began in the coal and steel companies, which were obliged by law, on revival after the war (for definite political reasons), to create secretly elected works councils and supervisory boards (on which workers were represented, with shareholders and independent persons) – the latter, in turn, to nominate the company management board. This practice was extended in 1972 to all companies, not just coal and steel, and all companies which employed more than five people had to have a works council. This scheme had, to begin with, several motives – among them, certainly, being to give to all a sense of joint responsibility, and to provide channels of information about decisions and problems. Employees are consulted on, but do not participate in, management decisions, save in coal and steel companies, where a worker has to be a member of the management. A new law in January 1972 – the Works Constitution Statute – extends the powers of the works councils to discuss wages, and even the power of veto over certain management decisions such as those relating to social and personnel matters.

These arrangements go further than anything arranged up till now in Britain, though other countries of the Community and, indeed, of EFTA have similar arrangements. In most continental countries employers are obliged to give to works councils prior information about changes in methods of production, new products, company organization and manning, and to receive at least as much information as that available to shareholders.

The consequences of these developments on the continent must have been to improve relations within industry between employer and employee, and must have been instrumental in achieving a more creative attitude to collective bargaining. Conditions of work, safety regulations, recreation facilities, even availability of lavatories and so on, have been better in consequence. These developments have made, therefore, a contribution not only to social harmony, but also to increased growth. They have a British equivalent in our various forms of joint consultation, whereby workers receive information and make suggestions: but consultation is not 'determination', and British workers, on the whole, do not receive information at the same level as those on the continent, and in particular not before the moment of implementation of the decision. The trend, too, even of advanced thought within the trade union movement is less towards participation of workers in particular enterprises as towards union participation. The question whether this is right is likely to be debated a good deal, once Britain is fully within the Community, particularly when such questions as the proposed European Company Statute come to be discussed further. (A draft statute for companies which operate in more than one country of the EEC was produced by the Commission in 1970. It has much in common with German practice, since it includes a works council and supervisory board.) It would be a great pity if the British Labour movement and Trade Union movement were to continue to vote against all these ideas from the point of view of principle – particularly since there are many multinational companies which would be affected. The development of British collective bargaining, and the relative lack of that within continental undertakings, is evidently related to the extent to which the continent have adopted forms of *Mitbestimmung* and we have not.

Once, after January 1973, the permanence of our membership of the European Community is accepted, the British trade union structure will probably bring itself to adapt towards action on a European scale. Obviously, this will be a complicated process, 'not without regrets and recriminations', as Ernest Mandel puts it in his *Europe versus America.* He adds, interestingly enough, that this might be accompanied 'initially by a further shift in the relationship of social forces to the disadvantage of the wage-earners. But if objective reality demands this restructuring and re-education of the labour movement, it would be ostrich-like to disregard it.'[27] Objective reality, in Mandel's sense, presumably means the onward drive of economic forces against which there can be no logical defence. In fact, however, what would most help in Britain would be the election to a few of the top jobs in the trade union movement of a series of younger and European-minded general secretaries.

Part III

1 The Economic Problem

'The economic motives that argued and still argue for the inclusion of Great Britain and the other states in the Common Market are obvious: a broader division of labour makes more possible rational production and a better system of distribution: intensive competition strengthens the dynamic forces ... Great Britain's entry [and that of the other EFTA countries] would raise the production and the economic capabilities of the EEC by more than half. Great Britain can demonstrate significant technical achievements in many areas: for instance, in space and air travel, rocket and atom technique, and computers. This 'know-how' within the Common Market would lead to a rapid heightening of productivity and Europe would be in a better position to maintain itself *vis-à-vis* the super powers.'

In these words, Willy Brandt summed up the economic advantages for Britain and for Europe of Britain's adhesion to the EEC, in the course of his book about foreign policy in 1968, just after the Labour government's abortive attempt to join the EEC in 1967. The simple statement is convincing. But it raises a large number of complicated questions.

The economic consequences of our entry into the European Community will be considerable, for better or worse. Firms manufacturing shoes, cotton, clothing, even ships and machine tools will be hard hit, though perhaps the first two of these are anyway doomed. Perhaps the Fiat or Renault and the Italian refrigerator or washing machine will overwhelm English competitors, in the classic manner of early capitalism, causing many more bankruptcies than we had anticipated, unemployment, suffering in regions, a sense of national inferiority and consequent political crisis. Perhaps too, Britain's low rate of growth over the last generation may have been less due to economics than to her geographical position; and Professor Kaldor argues that this aspect of things would apply even more in the future, and so cause the neglect of everything outside the central region of Western Europe, or inside the triangle formed by Milan, Dusseldorf and Birmingham.

It is impossible to guarantee absolutely against these dangers. But, if Britain were as weak as these comments suggest, the difficulties of her surviving as a major industrial and manufacturing country in the next generation would be great under any circumstances. It is true that, if we join the Community, many small firms may be damaged or have to merge; but, if we do not, large firms will be damaged, and those are firms upon which our prosperity, such as it is, depends. Any alternative (and these are discussed later on) would merely postpone the evil day.

By most sensible criteria, our long-term economic position is quite promising, always providing we have a larger economic base. As is also later suggested, Britain has the most capitalized and efficient agriculture in Europe. Our narrow financial possibilities within the Community are considerable. Reckoning the value of assets of companies, Britain has almost twice as much capital employed as there is in France, Germany and Italy put together, while the City does as much business in one day as all the European exchanges do in a week. London surprisingly re-emerged as the world's main financial centre during the 1960s, partly because of the growth of the Eurodollar market, and partly because more and more restrictions were imposed in New York in an effort to hold back the US deficit. Of the hundred largest businesses in the world in the 1960s, eleven were reckoned as British, only eighteen in the EEC as a whole. Traditional continental investors have invested in bonds, with fixed rates of interest, rather than in equity shares, where rewards have seemed either untrustworthy or unpredictable. This has meant too, that though much has been said by anti-

Marketeers about the likelihood of movements of capital away from Britain after our entry (the development of several investment trusts and unit trusts devoted to Europe underline this), there is also the likelihood of movements to Britain. British firms will be able to raise capital on the continent, as well as *vice versa*. Some movement to Britain has anyway begun from the continent, even from France: of particular significance may be the fact that in April 1972, several French companies, with a combined market value of £2,000M, began to seek a quotation on the London Stock Exchange, and, in May, the *Institut de Développement Industriel* announced its first 'overseas take-over' operation in financing the purchase by a French pharmaceutical company of a British marketing firm in this line of business.

QUOTED LIMITED COMPANIES IN EEC COUNTRIES
AND IN BRITAIN

	Number of quoted companies	Market capitalisation at 31.12.71 £'oooM	Equity turnover year to 31.12.71 £'oooM
Germany	550	13·3	1·7*
France	830	9·4	1·7
Italy	140	4·0	0·9*
Holland	400	5·3	1·3
Belgium	580	2·7	0·4
Total	2,500	34·7	6·0
United Kingdom	3,300	50·2	6·9

The City of London will obviously be important in the new Europe, though perhaps the assumption that it will inevitably be the centre of finance in Europe is a little bland. Still, British banks do far more business outside Europe than any continental ones do, sterling continues to finance 45 per cent of world trade and shipping, and European banks seem more likely to prefer

* year to 30.6.71 (*Guardian*, 28 April 1972)

London than Luxembourg, which was, in a sense, the financial capital of the European Community in its first fifteen years. London's insurance business is far bigger than that of any other capital in Europe.

A specially important point here is that over the last generation there is a sense in which the larger and more successful 'export-led' British firms have been too big for British boots; they have needed, as British capital has needed, as a political and economic base a community or a state larger than Britain has been able to provide.

These considerations should help to quieten the anxieties that Britain's economic position would be too weak to keep up, in a general way, within the Community. But a more serious doubt about our prospects seems to hover around some of the cultural or historical impediments to a real economic free market, even after 1978, when the transitional stage will presumably be over. The development of continental commerce and industry began, after all, in a quite different manner to that of Britain.

Let me take one very precise, even esoteric, example: the design and the standards of most British industrial plant are at least as high as that of their continental rivals. But much of British plant has been designed for an industry which scarcely exists in the Six, namely plant hire. This was the consequence of British governmental policies towards interest rates, which made it more attractive for customers to hire rather than to buy. Thus, in Britain today as the *Financial Times* has put it, 'no manufacturer of earth-moving equipment, mobile cranes, compressors ... or fork-lift trucks would dare to ignore the performance requirements of the hire fleets' – in particular, that the machines in question are easily transportable, and easily made ready for action.[28] This, for example, has meant that Britain has developed a special type of modern crane, which can travel at fifty miles an hour, and which is ready for full working within minutes of arriving at the site. But, outside the British hire business, there is little demand for these cranes, and the West European market for British designed equipment of this sort is, at the beginning, much less promising than the technical possibilities would warrant. Doubtless, in the long run, a market could be created, but that will demand salesmanship and verve for some years and, even given that, it is doubtful if a dent could ever be made in, for example, the relevant market in Italy, which is specially geared to the production of cheap and often bad equipment but for sale.

This extremely special argument applies in some ways, however, to the whole of transport. At present, 85 per cent of the freight in Britain goes by road, a percentage not approached by any other European country, and not nearly so by France or Germany which sends well under half by road. In both countries, as in the Netherlands, of course, even more, inland waterways still play a big part. But it is on the basis of experience of these proportions that the Community is clearly proposing to draw up its new long-term public policies towards transport, thereby naturally affecting severely the approximately 7 per cent of industrial costs which are caused by transport. Thus the lorries of Britain will have to conform with the EEC's existing laws – such as those restricting driving to eight to nine hours, excluding rest periods. There is also a Community rule requiring two drivers on any journey of over two hundred and eighty miles in a single day. All lorries will have to have a tachograph, measuring time, speed and distance – the so-called 'spy in the cab', such as Barbara Castle unsuccessfully tried to introduce a few years ago as compulsory. These changes would cost apparently at least £100M a year.

There are also several further proposals which the Commission has in mind. There is the fearful proposal for a new standard maximum weight limit of eleven tons per axle (compared to the present British limit of ten tons) which would apparently cost £200M on bridge replacement or reinforcement and, in order to save country villages from new persecution by noise, probably makes essential 'designated routes' for all heavy lorries. There is also the more extreme proposal for a Community licensing system, which would give control over haulage tariffs to the transport section of the

Commission – a severe clash with the present British system qualified only by the minimum standards of competence and safety. This is the direct reflection of the fact that, on the continent, road haulage began in the shadow of nationalized railway companies – governments financed most of the continental railways – and was severely controlled from the moment when, in the 1920s, roads began to be competitive. One consequence was that road haulage on the continent has remained mostly a matter of small businesses, with often one owner-driver. (Holland is an exception to this rule.)

This makes it likely that Britain's lorries and road haulage system will be constrained to follow a system which has a built-in preference for rail and water. This may increase costs, yet it suggests a development which can hardly be opposed on progressive grounds – unless indeed progressiveness is closely defined as nineteenth-century liberalism. 'Designated routes', for example, are quite a good idea. But the argument is not so much that here is something which the Commission wants to do: but that continental practice at the present springs out of past attitudes, or even traditions, which, irrespective of ideology, seem likely to affect British commercial chances within the European Community.

It may seem unfortunate that the most obvious first sign of the Community's undertakings in Britain should be this one: the thundering large continental lorry, rumbling along the roads like a detachment of tanks, may seem symptomatic of the clumsy juggernaut to which we seem to be attaching ourselves. It should be appreciated, however, that our entry into Europe will at least make it possible for us from within to try and restrict this development, on grounds of amenity or safety. There will be a British voice on the subject in Brussels. Otherwise, we should be faced with the painful choice of accepting continental practice; or of refusing it and, if so, damaging ourselves economically. The Community spokesmen incidentally have been at least as conscious of the environmental question in general as have our own.

Another unquantifiable though dissimilar problem relates

to the apparent dishonesty of some continental commerce. Standards of disclosure, for example, are very different from those of Britain or the US. Some Italian firms still produce three sets of figures – one for the tax office and the public, one for the business associates, and one, the only reliable one, for the directors. Italy indeed has to be excluded from most financial statistics because of poor data; spare money is usually despatched to Switzerland. The tradition in continental family firms towards secrecy is widespread. There is no pressure upon companies to show how they dispose of their assets. Attitudes to taxation on the continent are also variable. On the whole, however, this is a situation more likely to work to British advantage than the contrary, as it has probably worked towards German and Dutch advantage, so far as US investment is concerned. It is not, for instance, that a US firm wishing to invest is innately honest; nor that it necessarily likes 'to know where it is'; but that the sheer complexity of a less than straightforward attitude to taxation is baffling in a large US corporation where minor details are carefully scrutinized.

There are certain anxieties also over particular industries. There even remains uncertainty over the effect of entry into the EEC (actually, the ECSC) upon the steel industry. For example, British steel, at the moment, is below the German price and slightly below the French price. Britain will have to go over to a new system of pricing, by which, instead of all consumers in Britain paying a common price for steel wherever it may be delivered, they will have to pay the price as from certain 'basing points', together with the actual cost of delivery, which must also be specified. Before Britain joined the Community, a steel buyer in East Anglia would pay the same price for steel as one in Scotland, even if the steel had been produced in Scotland. From 1973 onwards, the 'true delivery cost' will have to be met – with, however, certain qualifications which the British government will presumably be able to insist upon, in the interests, for example, of Northern Ireland. The Commission will certainly also insist that the British government abandon any subsidies to the British Steel Corporation, thus, probably, forcing an increase in the price of steel by some 15 per cent. Fears about the sheer size of the BSC seem to be less on the continent than they were to begin with. But the European steel manufacturers are certain to insist on the Corporation's exposure to full competition.

Similar or relatively greater troubles affect (as suggested earlier) the paper industry. Here, the difficulties derive ultimately from Britain's previous membership of EFTA. That meant the abolition of tariffs against the world's major paper producers in Scandinavia. Cheaper Swedish products in particular caused damage to the English industry, and the closing of mills. That inheritance remains, with Britain's promise not to abandon her EFTA partners. The consequence is that British papermakers will probably not be able to compete within the enlarged Community until 1981.

Similar occurrences admittedly affected continental firms after the coming of the EEC. For example, the French refrigerator industry suffered severely after 1958, due to the tremendous success of the Italians in this sphere. The French government tried to protect its own by a variety of devices (such as a partly bogus insistence on certain 'standards') and indeed thwarted the Commission. Leaving aside, however, both the effect on agriculture of the political implications of the French behaviour (and the chances, probably remote, of similar British conduct) the overall advantages to the French economy of entry into the EEC has now been clear. French management has become far more efficient, French paternalism in industry has declined.

These problems, contingent upon entry into the European Community, in certain industries can, however, be balanced by the advantages for many others. Christopher Layton in his excellent study, *The Benefits of Scale for Industry,* points out that Europe is 'the only big market in the world whose consumers buy the type of medium and small sized car manufactured in Britain, and which offers the prospect of being completely open to British exports of . . . cars in the next twenty years'.[29] He points out how the US market is likely to be affected very seriously by Japanese competition; and how Commonwealth markets are increasingly protected by, for example, tariffs like Australia's 35 per cent tariff against British cars. At the same time, he suggests the many rationalizations possible in Europe, and achieved in the US, as a consequence of large scale operation: 'In the safety glass industry ... the basic processes are identical in America and Britain, but the variety of models in Britain over a much smaller output means a lower output per man, less automation of inspection and "batch feeding" of certain kinds of surface which, in America, would take a continuous flow.' There can be no doubt that the achievement of a single 'domestic market' for Europe in motor cars will benefit the industry considerably: perhaps even will be seen to have been essential in order to survive at all.

Similar beneficial consequences can be expected in heavy electrical industries, many specialized glass industries, chemicals, computers and so on. There have also grown up in the last ten years a series of industries which are beyond the means of national companies operating mainly in a single national European market: these include larger aircraft, communications satellite systems, nuclear reactors and certain sorts of computer.

It is also fair to add that as yet, even with the Community, there are some further obstacles to free trade within the Community. Social aids, such as free school milk, are naturally permitted. Aid to help regions is permitted. Aid to ship-building and some other declining industries has also been permitted, with some reluctance. But none of these things, obviously, would meet with hostility in this country, except from the Heath government, perhaps, in its first, and now abandoned, ideological stage. Governments too, perfectly obviously, within the Community, give preference to their own firms, particularly so far as building is concerned, but also in other sectors; and governments are the largest employers. Certain products (such as matches in France, Germany and Italy, and raw tobacco in France and Italy) are monopolies. Certain insistences on standards exist in the countries of the Community, some for safety reasons, some for what sound to be primarily traditional or aesthetic, some because of health.

There are also concentrations of economic power within the Community which prevent the advantages of free competition that develop in an integrated market. There are many sales syndicates to which nominally competing firms give full responsibility for marketing. Some of these are international. Gentlemen's agreements between national producers which are, in effect, cartels, and a number of other practices, such as the appointment of independent dealers in a particular country, lead to variations in price which distort, as the words of the EEC have it, the working of the Community. The most famous instance of this was the Grundig-Consten case. In this, the German firm of Grundig appointed Consten of Paris their dealer in radio and electronic equipment for France. But UNEF, Consten's rivals in France, obtained Grundig products from Germany and tried to sell them at lower prices. Balzac would doubtless have relished this situation. The Commission, to whom UNEF applied for help, did not. The European Court of Justice did not uphold the Commission's predictable ban on the whole agreement, but they did denounce the 'territorial protection' which Grundig had originally given to Consten.

All, however, that need be said is that existing practices have far from completed the arrangements for free competition, as they are also behind in respect of common policies, and that it will now be possible for the British to exert their influence to arrange the future of continental commerce more as they wish than would otherwise have been the case. The Community of the Six has constituted a powerful and, given the extraordinarily difficult circumstances of its first ten years (French obstructionism, in particular), remarkably innovatory system. With Britain a part of the Community, it will be responsible, as everyone knows, for over 40 per cent of the world's external trade – two and a half times more than that of the US, and nine times more than that of the Soviet Union. The opportunities should be very great.

2 Social Democracy and Economic Growth

The economic consequences of joining the Common Market are usually classified as of two sorts: the short term, or 'static', effects and the long term, or 'dynamic', effects. Economists who write of the desirability, or undesirability, of customs unions in general have long familiarized general readers with these two arguments: a version of them was current during the early years of the Zollverein in Germany in the 1820s and 1830s. The first would take into account such matters as changing from one set of tariffs (in this case the Commonwealth) to another; and the possibilities of both new 'trade creation' and 'trade diversion': these being convenient concepts to include the new industries likely to come into being; second, the new directions taken by old trading partners; and, third, the changes in trade undertaken by firms which have been used to trade in the Commonwealth. One can also perhaps add the elimination of risks which occur in transactions between different countries.

The real strength of the pro-marketeers' case rests on the likely dynamic, or long-term effects, of entry. These potential advantages are three: first, the likelihood of increased investment by British firms and foreign firms in Britain, if they are thereby ensured access to a larger market; secondly, increased efficiency through competition in a large market; and thirdly, the greater efficiency made possible because of the economies of scale in a market of some two hundred and fifty million people.

Many socialists will, however, say that it is all very well to suggest that the British economy, as at present constructed, may or may not be likely to prosper (given the bankruptcy of a grocer or apple farmer or two, who, after all, would vote Tory anyway) by one or other, or even all of these arguments; but, since the construction of this economy is wrong, the application to join the EEC cannot be regarded as anything more than a last gamble to save English capitalism: 'in general terms', writes a young Fabian, James Bellini, 'the dynamic of the European Community ... is diametrically opposed to the long-term interests of the mass of the population of that community' – and therefore, of our community too, because 'the economic dynamic of the Community is already clearly moving in the direction of supranational monopoly capitalism in which one more stage in the process of raising capital beyond all control of community forces is being completed'. (Since he wrote those words, however, Mr Bellini has joined Herman Kahn's Hudson Institute.)

This reasoning brings the argument to the question of what is today meant by social democracy. For this reason, the European debate affects, in a direct way, the question as to how far the original proposals of the fathers of socialism – the common ownership of the means of production, distribution and exchange, for example, as still defined in the existing Labour Party Constitution of 1917 – survive even as distant goals, or whether they have been replaced as political goals by other ideas. Today, it seems that, for every socialist who retains the old goals in his mind even as aspirations for the future, there is another who has modified them in the light of the experience acquired in the last twenty-five years. Such a person would now envisage not reluctantly, but gladly, that a mixed economy should last indefinitely – though limited, in the complicated variety of ways that all modern governments, even in time of peace, including even that of the USA, devise to ensure, as they hope, the community's interests.

The 'mixed society', admittedly, is not very well understood by socialists (or, in fact, by Conservatives either). The real point surely is that socialism in recent years has shifted from a discussion of means towards ends: the idea of nationalisation, for example, no longer occupies the centre of political argument within the Labour movement – despite the demand at the

Conference of 1971 for the nationalisation of banks, and the appearance, in the manifesto of 1972, of a demand for the nationalisation of development land. Socialists are today much more concerned with inequality, poverty, education, with improving the overall quality of the social services, with appreciating the needs of the community in new departures, such as playgrounds or neighbourhood amenity. Labour party conferences may still end with the singing of 'The Red Flag' and, only a little more than ten years ago, the Labour movement was divided over the desire of its then leader to make it more logical by removing the famous Clause 4 from its Constitution. But, even so, we are as much concerned now with diversity as with uniformity, and no longer see in nationalization a panacea – no longer perhaps can envisage panaceas as we used to. Nationalization, municipalization, the creation of state holding companies all have a part to play, but their introduction, or their abandonment, is not usually regarded as an article of faith. The nationalization of banks should be viewed on its merits in the light of the real benefits it might bring, as with the possible nationalization of development land. Doubtless all would agree that the community should, in emergency, control the 'commanding heights of the economy'. But control need not mean ownership, and emergency control need not mean permanent control. The problems furthermore within nationalized industries also have come to seem like those within all large undertakings, state-organized or privately owned.

It is also becoming evident that most of the money which will finance further social improvements must come from taxation: the financing even of continental insurance schemes seems likely to become more, rather than less, dependent upon the state. Therefore, the Labour movement has as much interest as any other organization in ensuring the profitability, within the margins which it should try and lay down, of all enterprises, private as well as public. Few, presumably, would cavil at seeing a partly government-owned company, such as BP, doing well within the European Economic Community. Ivor Richard and his friends have pointed out that, whether we like it or not, 'the standard of living of the British people does depend, in the last resort, on the export performance of the private sector of British industry'.[30] There is, admittedly, in the Treaty of Rome nothing against nationalization. How indeed could there be, when the public sector in the six old EEC countries is as significant as that in Britain? Italy nationalized her electricity supply industry after the coming of the EEC, and the German coal industry is now in a semi-nationalized state, while the French coal mines and electricity industry have long been state-owned. At the same time, the elaborate series of rules about competition and monopoly (particularly in Chapter 1 of Part III of the Treaty of Rome) go further towards the establishment of satisfactory guidelines for a mixed society than anything found in current British practice.

It is, furthermore, undeniable that no one really knows how the Labour movement will develop over the next few years. In 1971–2, it seemed to be leaning to what it is customary to regard as the Left: though it is doubtful whether proposals for the public ownership of banking should be regarded as radical. One cannot be certain that the real implications of such measures, within the mixed economy, have been properly explored. The problem of a much expanded bureaucracy such as has occurred over the last generation has scarcely been considered by any serious student of politics, except for Lord Balogh. A party which heads Left because of rhetoric, could head 'Right' for the same reasons, or for others, particularly if its leaders recall that they won the elections of 1964 and 1966 partly because they had given the appearance of modernity, of being open to new ideas, to 'the white heat of the technological revolution', as of governmental reform.

The Labour movement seems in fact to be still experiencing at the moment an intellectual crisis, a continuation of that which has affected it after its last spell in the government in 1951. The gap between idea (or programme) and action (or reality) seems great. Few wish to proceed towards revolutionary socialism, even if it were to be obtained, as it was by Allende in Chile, by democratic means. (Even if we leave aside questions of how Allende expects to maintain his administration in power, it is difficult not to conclude that Allende's socialism is democratic *faute de mieux*, rather than democratic as a matter of principle.) On the other hand, few accept the idea of bureaucratic, or meritocratic, technocracy. Most of such good research work as is being done is more on how more taxation should be spent by the state (as in the proposals included in *Labour and Inequality*, the Fabian Society's indictment of the last Labour government) than on how the economy can be made to grow to give the extra revenue required. The uncertainty during the last ten years over whether or not the country was going to join the Community has been one explanation for this general absence of serious discussion. Another has been the personalization of the issues by speculation over this or that leader's position.

For the purpose of this study, therefore, some assumptions are needed. My chief one is that the Labour movement will retain very roughly the general attitude to politics which characterized it in 1964, in the belief that it was not its plans and ideas which caused the relative failure of the Labour government of 1964–70, but the inability to put those plans and ideas into practice. This specifically means an interest in the efficient working of the mixed society within certain clearly defined margins, and with certain well defined social aims. This point of view, in fact, was implicit in *Labour and Inequality,* and even in most of the attacks made upon it. It was explicit in Anthony Crosland's famous Fabian lecture in 1971. It is even implicit in the point of view of those who thought that the Labour government 'failed' because it did not secure a structural revolution, or because the fundamental political assumptions which it made were wrong.

This last point is, in fact, a suitable moment to return to the point of departure from the main line of the argument, namely the discussion of the supposed economic effects, static or dynamic, of British entry into the Community.

3 An Economic Analysis

The 'static' effects of entry into Europe are essentially short-term effects deriving from changes in the use of existing resources following the liberalization of trade among member countries and the achievement of a common external tariff towards the rest of the world. Many economists and businessmen have made predictions and estimates. One of these sums was that of Professor John Williamson of the University of Warwick, one of the country's outstanding younger economists. He has estimated that the effects by 1978 of entry into the EEC upon English manufacturers could be calculated as follows – we would have 40 per cent more trade with the EEC, and 10 per cent more with associates of the EEC. Our trade with countries of the old EFTA who are not joining the EEC would drop by 10 per cent; and, with the Commonwealth, another 10 per cent. Trade with the rest of the world would remain much the same as it would otherwise have been. Our imports from the EEC would go up by 45 per cent and from the Commonwealth and EFTA down 7 per cent. Our imports from the rest of the world, however, would go up by 5 per cent. Professor Williamson admitted that these estimates were guesses, and the only things of which he could really be certain were that entry into the EEC would 'provoke a substantial increase in two-way trade with the existing members of the EEC', and that 'the effects on the industrial trade balance will be rather minor'.[31] All this seems, with all due respect, to be banal; as Professor Williamson probably would be happy to agree. None the less it seems likely that at least no decline to overall trade is

E

likely, and Professor Williamson calculates that, with regard to GNP, a small increase would probably take place in growth as a result of the changing trade pattern. It is easy both to question these figures, as being absurdly schematic, and to pooh-pooh the very modest conclusions that he draws. Still, the mere fact that the conclusions are not negative in an area where many economists have been so is a matter of the greatest importance.

Now for the arguments based on the likely dynamic effects of entry. First, there is the possibility of greater investment as a direct result of membership. In Britain today, despite many assets (some of which, as argued later on, are bound to have a critical effect in the future), there is a desperate need for investment. This somewhat panicky adjective is justified, so far as short-term matters are concerned, by the scandalous unemployment figures of 1970–2 and, so far as long-term questions are concerned, by the slow rate of growth.

British firms will certainly increase investment in consequence of our adherence to the EEC. In 1971, for example, the *Guardian* carried out a survey of two hundred leading firms of Britain (*Guardian,* 12 June 1971). About half said that, if we were to join the EEC, they would increase their investment on the continent, and 22 per cent said that they would do so in Britain. These figures might seem to confirm the fear that our entry into the Market would cause an unacceptable outflow of capital. But those who will invest on the continent include in their considerations a good deal of 'follow-up' upon past investments, such as services, or 'after sales' investment. Some of these investments would be financed by raising capital on the continent, in which case no movements of capital would be involved. (If all such finance were raised on the continent, there would be a direct long-term benefit in the form of dividends and profits that would come to Britain.) In this category, perhaps, might be placed Leylands' purchase of Innocenti Morris in Milan, and half the plant at Pamplona. Future investment is more likely to be concentrated in Britain, where the main plant, and the top management, is concentrated. If we had not joined the Community, incidentally, many in the latter might perhaps have moved to the continent. (Some figures on long-term capital flows in EFTA incidentally, show that the three most significant EFTA countries reduced their rate of investment in each other.[32]) Furthermore, even the 22 per cent who said that they would invest in Britain represents a big increase in total investment.

Representatives of the motor car industry have calculated that that branch of the economy will have increased their investment by 6 to 9 per cent by 1980, or by £10M to £20M, over and above what would otherwise probably have occurred. This will doubtless be reflected in motor car component industries. Perhaps this would be a matter of additional or extra, investments of £120M by 1980, or £260M by 1985. Such investments might, it is thought, have the effect of increasing, by 1978, the growth of the British GNP by 0·5 per cent.[33] As for foreign investments here, Britain may have lost many US investments by failing to join the Community earlier; but it is likely that future US investments will be established to a large extent in Britain in preference to continental countries. Much of Ford's (and other US) investment in Germany and in France might have gone to Britain had it not been for the Americans' understandable desire to avoid tariffs. In 1971, about one quarter of the hundred and sixty or so leading US firms with European subsidiaries said that they expected to expand in Britain following entry into the EEC. Other surveys of the same sort point to the same conclusion. This is less a matter of the 'special relationship', now obsolete, but of language, ease of arrangement and, perhaps, a for the moment higher standard of civic morality in matters of tax. As mentioned earlier, London practice on the stock exchange insists upon, and obtains, more strict accounting requirement than, for example, Paris does. In France, companies seek to conceal profits as much as they can, because honesty only adds to tax charges, and does little to increase their ability to raise cash. Similar comments can be made about Italy. The German market is honest, but its stock exchange smaller than that of Britain.

Investment is not a matter where exact prediction is possible.

It derives from moods, hunches and appreciation of the psychological possibilities for growth, as is evident from the slightest acquaintanceship with a really successful businessman. A discussion of why particular investors favoured this or that undertaking at a particular time occurred during the tribunal on the Bank Rate leak in 1957.* It threw an odd light on the motives of stockbrokers. But, by and large, the belief is widespread that investments in Britain will increase after 1 January 1973. That fact is in itself an optimistic sign.

It is here important to distinguish between long-term capital movements, or investments, and short-term ones. It is the latter about which Harold Wilson was, rightly, concerned in his speech at the Labour party's special conference and earlier. These exchange, or speculative, flows, or flows in response to different interest rates, are theoretically made easier under Articles 67 to 73 of the Treaty of Rome, which envisage free mobility of capital within the Community, and the currency crisis of 1972 might seem a foretaste of evil things to come. But the role of the pound as an international currency has declined. International support for the pound was formalized by the Basle Agreement achieved by Roy Jenkins when chancellor. Articles 73 and 109 of the Treaty of Rome include safeguards enabling members of the Community to take protective action during a crisis – as France did in 1968 after the *événements*; and the Werner Plan for monetary union (to be discussed later) implies the irrevocable fixing of the parity ratios which will prevent intra-European exchange speculations; and a stabilization fund to help member states who are in difficulty.

On the whole, a general reading of the economic work done on investment in consequence of British adhesion to the Community seems likely to be over-cautious. A more important question relates to where that investment is liable to be estab-

---

* In 1957, certain interests made money out of the increase in the Bank Rate through being informed beforehand as a result of their official position in the Bank of England. The subsequent public enquiry threw a lot of interesting light on City practices.

lished. There is an obvious chance of excessive concentration in particular sectors to the cost of others.

A second point, in the list of favourable dynamic implications, is the likelihood of increased efficiency through competition – an argument which was, for the first few years of the controversy over the Market, the main one. Today, these arguments seem less appealing. Tariffs are now quite low anyway. The philosophical approach does not seem to fit the reality: what is 'competition' in the age of oligopoly? The implications for industries in the old EEC were never statistically worked out. Existing large firms will however certainly be able to grow larger in the European Community, without the evils of monopoly. Small, efficient firms will benefit if they are responsible for a specialized product and if they are, at the moment, faced with a small demand, because of the limited home market. A 'jolt' can be given, by dropping tariffs on imports, though some believe that Britain, since the Restrictive Practices Act of 1956, has been more effectively anti-Trust than the continent. But what happens to those who work in the 'sub-optimal' sectors which, according to most predictions, will suffer? Are we sure, for example, that we wish to see the end of all cosy village shops, and to replace them with 'one stop' supermarkets? This is a point of some sociological, psychological and, hence, political importance: much of European urban life is dry and without much sense of community. Hence many of its problems, and its crimes. The destruction of neighbourhoods, in the interests of redevelopment, creates criminals almost equal in number to those who are dispossessed. The many little Bloomsbury shops in Great Russell Street are 'sub-optimal' firms due to be removed for the building of the new British Library. They nevertheless serve the community in a different way (and a creative way) to the beautiful tower which Lord Eccles has assured us will displace them. The same is true of many small shops whose significance society is apt to overlook, as it does that of barrows in markets, partly because they do not figure significantly in the statistics – particularly if they evade taxation.

Still, this argument of increased growth from competition has undoubtedly some validity. The way to safeguard against consequential disruption is to make exceptions to the rules, not to refuse to implement the rules. Furthermore, though we must regret the disappearance of such shops and their similar undertakings, we should regret even more the disruption caused by the disappearance of village schools whose contribution to neighbourhoods is for obvious reasons far greater.

Then there is the third argument about economies possible from greater scale or size of operations. A larger market naturally increases the possibilities here. One of the reasons for the swift growth of the US economy after the end of the Civil War was the fact that US industrialism was able to develop within a continental economy. This has also been one of the reasons for the continuing expansion since then. The domestic home market of the old European Economic Community is five times larger than Britain's, and has been growing twice as fast as our own over the last few years – whatever the precise reason. A market of such a size stimulates the mass production of many cheaply priced goods. Longer production runs should be possible. Enterprising firms would be able to achieve many economies. Our most important export industries, particularly our science-based, or technology-based, industries, should thus find a very large home market, together with great opportunities to invest, and to expand. If this were to be accompanied by better, and more stable, industrial relations, delivery dates should be easier to meet, and customers therefore easier to please. This will affect all companies, particularly specialist firms.

That a great potential exists for utilizing economies of scale in the European Market has been shown by numerous studies. Ford UK, for example – if an example from the motor industry yet again is permissible – estimates that an investment of £100M is needed each year. In order to make such large investments possible, two million vehicles have to be sold each year, including half a million of a popular model. Clearly, the UK home market is too small to allow this, and prior to joining the Community the outlook was black, in view of the decline in

Commonwealth preferences, as Australia and other ex-colonies attempted to stimulate their own production of motor vehicles. At the same time, access to the Community market was restricted by tariffs of 11 per cent to 22 per cent.

These arguments hold for most modern industries, especially those of an advanced technological nature like aerospace and computers. It is significant that these two industries, together with motor vehicles, petro-chemicals and heavy electrical equipment, may account for 40 per cent of the UK's total output by 1980. Thus greater economies of scale in these industries will have a major impact upon the economy as a whole. Other industries for which excellent predictions were being made in 1972 included those making non-ferrous metals, transport equipment of many kinds, metal manufactures.

It may be argued that this point only benefits capitalism – Ford UK is, after all, not the most egalitarian of enterprises. The argument about economies of scale, about greater growth generally, should, however, be seen in the wider context of the arguments about the European-level control of multinational companies and monopolies generally, of the development of trans-national Trade Unions, and of a greater attention to the social costs of economic growth; and economies of scale can equally well be exploited by nationalized industries.

It seems improbable that the economic arguments about the desirability of our accession to the Common Market can ever be satisfactorily resolved if they are confined to predictions about increases, or decreases in trade or in economic growth. The conclusion of Professor Williamson on these subjects is however worth quoting:

'I fall in the category of those who originally believed that the case for entering Europe was entirely political, and that the economic effects were unlikely to be of much consequence in either direction. The advent of the CAP prevented one taking refuge in this cosy belief: in the absence of significant benefits from industrial free trade, entry would clearly impose an economic cost. The question of whether free trade with Europe would bring gains could no longer be brushed aside. . . .'

He then described how, first, 'the finding that the ratio of export to domestic prices is closely related to the rate of growth of exports', and how, secondly, a study by two US economists (R. J. and P. Wonnacott) on the effects on Canada of a free trade area with the US, had caused him to reach, in the end, a much more positive conclusion: 'it remains true that any assessment of the overall benefits contains a strong element of guesswork. My central guess would be something in the region of [an increase of] one half per cent from each of the three extra sources identified (economies of scale, competition, investment) giving a total of $1\frac{1}{2}$ per cent on GNP by the end of the transition.'[35] This careful estimate does not of course go very far, but an increase of the order suggested is certainly not one to be ignored in a country whose low growth rate has been so notable during these last years.

The economic arguments would have to be overwhelmingly negative for us to reject entry on these grounds if the basic soundness of the political background is accepted. They are not, and, in certain particular and important ways, very far from being so. This becomes clear on consideration in particular of three further critical matters: the multinational company; technology; and a European currency.

4 The Multinational Company

The question of how to approach the multinational company, the phenomenon of the last generation, should be at the new heart of the pro-Market case within the socialist movement. Put briefly, it is impossible now to build a socialist Britain outside the European Community, since capital, swifter to innovate than its enemies, is already internationally organized. The only alternative would thus seem a 'Socialist Europe' – including the control of capitalism at what would, in the past, have seemed an international level.

The first point to be noted is that internationally organized capitalism can now play off regions and countries against each other. A powerful company can try and thwart national regional policies by insisting on establishing new plant in prosperous regions. The same may occur in respect of policies over pollution.

Second, such a company can also play off workers in one country against those of another. If there is a climate of strikes in one country, the skilful internationalist can change production to another one. Henry Ford made this point brutally, in a speech in 1971, but managers of Ford-Argentine, and Ford-Genck (Belgium) and even Ford-Dagenham had made the point before. Such decisions can also be made if a company finds that costs of labour are too great in a particular country: the board can decide to switch production to an area of low labour costs: Courtaulds has thus already moved part of its undertakings from South Wales to Northern Spain.

Third, multinational companies are able to undermine

national economic policies and controls in many other ways: in particular, they have become the real experts in tax avoidance, by using the device of transferring profits to the country of the lowest, or the most easily avoided, tax. This is a particular problem when the Western world is facing an ethical crisis over questions of taxation in general. These companies are also able to affect a country in which they have invested by 'transfer payments' to shareholders and by reinvestments of profits in other countries, as well as accentuating monetary crises by intra-company changes in currencies, as, for example, is believed to have been done by the Volkswagen Company in 1971. US (and other firms) have often been known to take decisions favourable to their home rather than to their host – such as closing efficient branches in the second, rather than inefficient ones in the first. Remington Rand seem to have done this in Lyons in 1962, and General Motors in Paris in 1962. Multinational companies also favour their home base – almost always the US, in this respect – rather than their host in respect of research and development. A Stanford Research Institute Report showed a few years ago that, while half a sample of two hundred leading US firms undertook some research in Europe, most spent less than 4 per cent of their budget for this purpose there, even though that 4 per cent might account for more than that spent altogether by their British competitors.

There are also problems of scale in multinational companies, which are not so easy to quantify. The US colossus, IBM, has a turnover greater than the budgets of many countries. The psychological and political consequences of IBM's operations can be considerable. Such undertakings may be able, or one day be able, to blackmail countries through their customers. The process, after all, is far from complete: as is seen by recent European mergers between, for example, the tyre kings of Britain and Italy, Dunlop and Pirelli, the steel producers Hoesch and Hoogovens, CII, Siemens and Philips, the French, German and Dutch electrical (including computer) giants.

It may, however, seem that this argument conflicts with that which suggests that, among the benefits which can be expected to accrue from accession to the EEC, are 'the economies of scale'. On the contrary, what is being argued here is the necessity of supranational political action to prevent monopoly and to defend regions, or even countries, from the consequences of these actions; and by the development of effective international trade unions. Action of the sort already undertaken by the Commission against Europeanballage* is certainly easier within the Community. Neither governmental nor trade union action would be out of the question if taken outside the EEC, but they would obviously be more easy. 'If we were members of the EEC', said Mr Roy Mason in the House of Commons in March 1970, when President of the Board of Trade, 'we could ... join in the establishment of the European Company Statute and the setting up of an institutional framework to supervise the European Company.'

It is undesirable to be totally negative about the multinational company. Insofar as it is a new grouping of men and women, with loyalties to an international or supranational organization, it has much to commend it in an age which has seen the discrediting of the nation state with a few, largely accidental, exceptions. The 'steady attrition of political power, and the maximization of private power, at the level of multi-national, and hence supranational control', in the words of one of its enemies, James Bellini, is not a wholly evil development in a generation which has seen the maximization of public power brutally misused too. Anything which challenges the nation state has something to commend it. (What is to be regretted, perhaps, is that international companies are not really properly international for, under the guise of multinational action, they are usually controlled from national boardrooms in, say, New York or Detroit.) Furthermore, the international company is performing one essential service: of staking out a new agenda for, in the long run, collective activity. It would be impossible, for example, to nationalize these companies; but some could perhaps be Europeanized in one way or another and run for

* See page 150.

the collective profit, under the Commission. (Indeed, a pilot undertaking of this sort ought to be tried as soon as possible.) Furthermore, the international company seems likely to be one of the institutions which are certain to help to prevent any incipient US-European trade war from turning into anything more serious.

We may very well see established, in the near future, two or three hundred multinational companies, not responsible to any particular government, and together responsible for a great proportion of international trade. Many of these will, of course, be US-based. They will be multinational in the sense that they are incapable of acting within a normal nation. Their existence impels the enlargement of an effective European Economic Community almost more than any other argument. Similarly, it will be easier when within Europe to make an effort to supervise the vast amounts of money which pass through the Eurodollar market, which has so preoccupied the City in the 1960s and the early 1970s.

5 Technology

Similarly compelling arguments arise in respect of technology, so far as Europe is concerned. European technological possibilities are clearly greater with Britain within the European Community than with her outside it, and so are British. It would be tempting to say that this would be so regardless of what happened to the economy, but that would be frivolous, considering the importance of technology in the British economy. In 1971 Arthur Bottomley pointed this out, at Labour's Common Market Conference: 'The Germans invented the rocket, and the British invented radar. Why were we not able to harness these inventions? Because we were fragmented, with no economic resources, or strength, to back developments.' That, indeed, has been a characteristic European scientific development of the last generation. Atomic energy was a supreme example of a European invention being exploited in the US. It is doubtless unfortunate that this, and other major achievements which could have been creatively used in Europe (since 1945, that is), should not have been so, thanks to disunity; and there are hundreds of minor technological developments of the same sort, whose benefit to Europe has either been late, or has occurred in the shape of 'Americanization'. Even among studies of European integration, US scholars have been in the forefront: in Europe, political science is still, in comparison, in what one French team of social scientists referred to as 'l'état artisanal'. These arguments are familiar to Harold Wilson, who used them himself several times during his justification of his application to join the EEC in 1967: with the best will in the world, it is difficult to forget his demand that we create a 'European technological community' to avoid becoming 'industrial helots' subservient to the US or to the Soviet Union. A particular interest should be attached to the scheme for a European technological community, since it would obviously demand a sophisticated blend of ideas within the mixed economy, which would themselves lead inevitably, and pragmatically, as Harold Wilson would have said, to greater integration and the pooling of sovereignty. The position here is not so much a matter of the 'brain drain' to the US or even of the drain of ideas, but of the penetration by the US of British or continental companies: in 1965, US companies had, it seems, penetrated 80 per cent of the computer production of the European Community, 25 per cent of the motor industry, 15 per cent of synthetic rubber and 10 per cent of petrol chemicals; since that time the proportion has grown substantially.

There is doubt about the significance of such statistics. To assume simply that such foreign investment damages national interest is absurd, as any student of nineteenth-century US history would point out, as would all realists. Foreign capital becomes a danger to independence only at a certain definite, if not easily measurable, point. Even so strong an opponent of the principle of US 'imperialism' as Ernest Mandel has denied (in *Europe versus America*) that US imperialism is taking over Western Europe wholesale – though admittedly, Monsieur Mandel has his own reasons for this reticence, since he has a very sharp axe to grind with the European bourgeoisie.

Until now, the various plans for developing European technology have been hampered by the reluctance of member states of the old EEC to grant to the Communities the necessary legal powers. That has not prevented ideas being put forward for, for example, an Industrial Reorganization Corporation (IRC) on a European level, and for a Community budget of $2000M for 'industry, science and technology' by 1980.[36] Britain has a special interest in such matters since industries of an advanced technological nature will account for such substantial proportion of our manufacturing by 1980: thus even a small increase in their output per man, as a result of economies of scale, would have a major impact on the economy as a whole. The Labour government's white paper on the European Community made this point quite clearly: 'the future of the so-called high-technology industries – in the rest of Western Europe just as much as in the UK – depends decisively on whether or not it proves possible to create an enlarged Community.'

The aerospace industry is an obvious example of a series of undertakings that would greatly benefit from a European approach, partly because of an enlarged home market and partly because of the need to share Research and Development. Aerospace also proves the inadequacy of a bilateral basis, as the fate of the Concorde suggests. The history of that aircraft has two morals: first, the rising costs, which show a lack of co-ordination and a failure to achieve real economies of scale: and second, there is no home market of a size large enough to enable an undertaking of this size immediately to pay its way.

This argument can be exaggerated through excess of zeal. Europe may perhaps turn out, in future, to be more a consumer society, with less emphasis on investment, public or private, than either the US or the Soviet Union. For it is possible that the age of European inventiveness is at an end, with the innovations of the future less probable here than in other countries. But this might, in fact, make co-operation more desirable than ever. It may even be that we might become, for once, a community able to implement the ideas of others: for example, learning from the lesson of Westinghouse and Tenneco, the Community may build their projected giant nuclear power station on an offshore floating centre. (The Commission has already asked the Technische Hochschule of Aachen to look at the practical possibilities of building a plant twenty times the size of the biggest power station operating in Britain.)

One other question immediately arises: that is, what form of collaboration, if any, should a Europe united on a technological basis have with other superpowers, such as Russia or the US? For example, what attitude should the new Europe have towards collaboration with the US in space? This is an area of modern technology where even the US cannot afford the full costs. An early decision is, indeed, necessary on this subject, since the US is beginning a whole new stage in its space programme. This 'post-Apollo' stage envisages not a specialized project with a limited objective, but a general method of space transport, which Europe may wish to use. The US seems to want European collaboration, in respect of some sharing of costs. £200M has been mentioned as a 'minimum investment as their fee for a piece of the main shuttle programme'.

The implication of remaining indefinitely outside these projects might be seriously damaging to Europe's long term technological position. For example, we might be kept outside all questions of weather control, a serious possibility within the next generation. (Weather control resembles a kidney machine on a large scale: at least in the early stages there will be political priorities in deciding who will have the benefit.) The desirability of a European commitment along these lines seems to outweigh the disadvantages, on balance, since a foot in this advanced technological field must be beneficial, in the long run. Obviously, this is a field where Britain alone would be quite incapable of making any worthwhile contribution at all. In this respect, as in some others, Japanese experience is helpful. The Japanese computer industry, for example, seems to have been able to profit from US technology without US domination. On the whole, it is probable that 'the political significance of advanced technology' (Christopher Layton's words again) implicitly or explicitly was the driving force behind the applications of both Labour and Conservative governments to join the Community at all. All the arguments point to entry and to greater opportunities being available in consequence.

6 Monetary Union

There has been one other subject lingering behind these diverse arguments on the economic validity, or the reverse, of British entry into the European Economic Community: money. To most people, the word 'economic', so far as it applies to their private pockets, means how such-and-such is going to be financed. Similarly, the millstone around the neck of the last Labour government was sterling. Every time there was a crisis, people who held sterling sold it, and so made the crisis worse than it need have been. Some discussion has already occurred here of the effect of entry into the Community on 'short term capital flows'. In the European Community, the burden of sterling will be effectively sloughed off. Within a few years, further steps will probably have been made towards a European monetary system. Some headway, in consequence of that alone, may be possible towards the achievement of a rational and progressive world monetary system. Here, as in some other ways, British entry into the Community could make a major contribution, not just towards the resolution of British problems, but towards those of the world.

There are now two main proposals for the development of a European monetary system: first, the Werner proposals, providing for a European monetary union by 1980, linking together existing currencies into a multi-currency area with complete interconvertibility and irrevocably fixed rates. This was warmly commended by Harold Wilson, when still prime minister, at a meeting of the TUC in 13 January 1970. The second proposal, made by a Federal Trust study group, is for the creation of a

'Europa' currency to exist alongside national currencies. This would probably be better, since it would leave national currencies free, for the time being, to fluctuate alongside the Europa money for perhaps a long interim period, and so allow the adjustments which would be necessary in exchange ranges. There is also a third, less likely, if simpler plan to take one of the existing currencies of the Community, such as the Pound or the Mark, as the 'European' common currency.

Some steps have however already occurred which suggest that the first proposal is the most likely one to be adopted. The fixing of exchange rates, the elimination of margins of fluctuation in the established rates against the dollar, and a ban on both devaluations and revaluations, is recommended as the first step towards a realization of the Werner plan; and, in consequence, in May 1972 the European currencies were held to a margin of $2\frac{1}{4}$ per cent in respect of what they could fluctuate against each other (a scheme quickly damaged by the 'floating' of the pound a month later). A committee under Monsieur Camille Bruck, director of the Luxembourg finance department, was formed to co-ordinate economic policies, and a report by Treasury and Central Bank officials has been circulated on the subject of monetary union.

The Federal Trust supporting the second, Europa project, has proposed too that a European bank, to pool part of member states' reserves, should be established as soon as possible. This is an improbable eventuality, but the proposal for a European currency is one of the most important parts of EEC policy. It has however been strangely ignored in the 'great debate' though Mr Callaghan expressed the warmest approval for the idea in 1967, when still chancellor of the exchequer, ('certainly we in the UK are ready to make our contribution to the closest possible European co-operation in these matters which can bring nothing but good to all our peoples'). Mr Wilson certainly had this view in 1970.

In the short term, the idea presents several clear advantages and one distinct disadvantage. The advantages are that monetary union would abolish inter-European speculation over exchange rates. It would make possible the pooling of reserves. It would give the European monetary market the cohesion that it needs to avoid further dependence on the dollar. It would save endless time and trouble by assimilating, in character and risk, international transactions to domestic ones. It would also provide greater efficiency for control over multinational companies.

The development of the international company has made it clear that the traditional boundaries of the European states do not any more coincide with the boundaries of a currency area. The disadvantages are that problems arising from the balance of payments will no longer be able to be resolved by devaluation. (The French devaluation of 1969 was a shock even then and would be impossible with a real common currency and so would the British action in 1972.) If the problem were a short term one, reflecting deficiencies of inter-EEC payments, the question could be easily enough resolved by a common fiscal or monetary policy – if indeed there were to be one: the procrastination on the subject in the Council of Ministers is considerable. If it is a long term problem, the consequence of historical factors not easily resolved, related to trade union attitudes or the industrial structure generally, the difficulties arising from an adverse balance of trade would be greater. A really dynamic regional policy would be essential in these circumstances. Otherwise, there would be a serious danger of local unemployment, a decline in regional investments, and economic stagnation. Such strong policies as would be needed imply evidently the need for strong political institutions, which will co-ordinate fiscal and monetary policies, since monetary union can only achieve the beneficial results desired if an economic union is worked out at the same time.

The long term significance of the proposal for monetary union is thus enormous. A common currency and a common monetary reserve would give to the Community the power, if it chose to use it, to impose its economic and most of its political decisions. The common currency might provide the cement of the new European society, filling a role which, in the past, might have been fulfilled by police forces, or by armies. It is certain to be one of the main preoccupations of the next ten years.

These possibilities should obviously be considered against the fact that the world economic situation has radically changed since the time of Britain's first application to join the Community, indeed since Britain's subsequent applications. Since August 1971, the US has been no longer able, or willing, to act as the ultimate guarantor of world currencies. It will be replaced, doubtless in the short term, by a world reserve unit, growing out of the existing system of Special Drawing Rights. The subsequent devaluation of the dollar has altered the economic situation of the world for the first time since Bretton Woods. In these circumstances, it scarcely needs an economist to show how much more desirable it is to be a part of a continent-wide monetary bloc than to be an overstretched old nation. But we should also bear in mind that a full European currency, with a Federal Reserve system (which the Governor of the Bank of England has described as an objective), will be difficult to achieve unless there are common fiscal policies as well as regional ones. Indeed the 'floating' of sterling in June 1972 showed yet again the impossibility of achieving Monetary Union without the necessary accompanying economic measures, particularly a strong regional policy. The control of short-term capital flows would presumably be much easier if there were a full monetary union. The 'crisis' of 1972 was, in fact, primarily speculative in character, perhaps deriving from the advice of London brokers to continental clients to diversify their equity portfolios.

7 A Europe of Regions

During this discussion of the economic consequences of our association with Europe, and of the main strategic advantages that this will offer in respect of currency matters, technology and relations with the multinational company, one general problem has frequently cropped up, but has been put aside, since it seemed too large a one to deal with simply in passing. This is the question of regional policies under the European Community. It has been suggested, for example, that the devices of the Regional Employment Premium and of the Industrial Development Corporation, introduced by the Labour government and dropped by the Tories, would be impossible under the Treaty of Rome. In practice, however, that is not so: the Community's member countries' regional policies have been at least as progressive as ours, particularly since 1970. Mr Harold Wilson himself pointed out, in May 1967, that the Community had begun to use regional policies whose progressiveness he did not doubt, even though he had not contemplated their introduction in England: these measures included 'differential pricing of publicly owned industries and services to encourage regional development, and a variety of incentives, including investment grants, tax reliefs, . . . and cheap long-term loans to encourage mergers'. France has introduced an INI which is similar to our now abandoned IRC. Control of development in the Paris and Lyons areas has been strong. In Italy, some £900M is spent a year on development of backward areas, compared with £250M to £300M in Britain. There is also a traditional use of public enterprise, such as the ENI or IRI, to help regional investment. Since 1950, 40 per cent of new Italian state investment has had to be in the South, and recently even more. These investments have, incidentally, provided a good example of the possibilities of collaboration between private enterprise and the state in a mixed economy: the former have provided the industries, the state the 'infrastructure', specially tailored to the needs of the firm. (This has also occurred in France.) In both Italy and France, there has been an integration of national and regional planning of considerable importance, partly based on the idea of the 'growth pole'* (which has also been supported by a Labour study group). (One of the first big schemes, incidentally, the Bari-Taranto-Brindisi growth axis, was started on the inspiration and help of the European Commission.) Germany used, for political reasons, to lay less emphasis upon regional planning, but she has nevertheless developed a wide-ranging policy on this subject through the *'Regionale Aktionsprogramme'*.

The European Community itself has not evolved a policy which responds to the necessity of ensuring that the regions outside the extremely prosperous centre do as well as they should. But so far as national policies are concerned, scarcely any restrictions are implied in present Community regulations. The only qualification is that aids in central-aid areas should not exceed 20 per cent of the total investment cost of each project – and no limit elsewhere. Belgium's recent action in trying to declare virtually the whole country a development region was also understandably not permitted. (The Belgian action was itself determined by indecision over the line dividing Walloon from Flemish interests, and a governmental reluctance to take responsibility.)

At the same time, a Community regional policy is obviously needed, partly in consequence of the Mansholt agricultural

---

* The idea of the growth pole was developed by F. Perroux, the French economist, and in practice embodies the suggestion that, within regional areas needing development, specially promising areas should be selected for investment and therefore investment aids. A 'growth pole' could be either urban (e.g. Lille) or industrial (e.g. underdeveloped areas such as Bari-Taranto).

plan which proposes the reshaping of landholding; partly, in consequence of the reforming of the European Social Fund; partly, because of the enlargement of the Community, with new and critical areas, all slightly different from continental ones, such as the British north, the north of Denmark, the south of Eire and so on; and most important, because of the schemes for monetary union which strongly demand regional policies to be effective.

A community merely designed to increase competition would obviously affect regional questions severely. Inefficient industries would be expected to suffer. What if they happen to be the only source of employment to hundreds of people in a poor area? Mobility of labour cannot be assumed: 'workers' are people, or families, not statistics only, who may not desire to move, or who may not have the will, much less the expertise, to acquire new knowledge in the best centres of retraining.

British regional problems also differ from those of the continent in that our declining industrial areas are the critical ones, whereas the Community is in general geared towards depression in, and underdevelopment in, agriculture. We are not, however, alone here: Lorraine, the Franco-Belgium coalfield and the Ruhr are industrial, with some of the same sort of difficulties of adaptation encountered in the British shipbuilding or coal mining areas. In consequence, Germany sympathises with the British view on these matters. The French seem to suggest that the CAP was, in a sense, a concession by the other countries to France in return for the latter remaining a part of the Community at all in De Gaulle's day. They would also point out that Britain would obviously gain substantially, at everyone else's cost, if declining industrial areas were treated as backward agricultural ones are.

Similar judgements can be made in respect of the Community's institutions for the retraining, and the redeployment, of those who are driven out of industry because of the exhaustion of resources such as coal. The Social Fund of the Community, the Guidance and Guarantee Fund, and the Coal and Steel Community Fund are provident institutions which guarantee retraining facilities for redundant workers similar to (if as yet smaller in scale than) the Labour government's arrangements. The first of these had a budget of some $100M in 1972, a sum which was to be increased to $250–300M per annum in future: the fund is financed by the member states in proportion to riches. The sum is far too small, but it is most probable that the fund could be helpful in respect of declining British industries. The fund does not, however, concern itself with propping up such industries; only with those affected by structural change. Programmes of industrial retraining should be complementary to regional policies, since they should not be a policy of their own (as envisaged in the Conservative budget of 1972) and should not involve undue migration from the home region.

The regional problems of Europe are among the most intricate, but so are the possibilities among the most interesting. First, generous regional policies will be found to be among the most important in enabling corrections to be made, in the name of equity, to European policies which might otherwise turn out unjust. An extreme example of this might be the consequences of the adoption of a European monetary policy making devaluation impossible. Second, regional preoccupations will probably have the beneficial effect of breathing new life into such neglected areas as Aquitaine, Wales, Sicilia or the German Eifel at the cost of prestige of the nation states along their old boundaries, states which were subsequent historically, to the regions themselves. Already, this has occurred in a country such as Italy, whose diversity was damaged by the needs of the unitary state. Perhaps, in the future, the nineteenth-century concept of Italia will, in consequence of a larger one, come to seem as parochial as the Kingdom of Naples has seemed since 1870, while old Neapolitan considerations will revive. (As Denis Mack Smith and other historians have pointed out, the Risorgimento benefited the few at the probable cost of the many.) A 'Europe of regions' indeed, is an attractive idea to those who would prefer to deliver politics from the centralizing pomposity, and frequent inhumanity even in time of peace, apparently inseparable from national democracies. Michel Philipponneau has also pointed out that a 'Europe of regions' is more likely to achieve the psychological changes necessary for a creative policy towards the aesthetic and local problems of the environment,[37] and John Pinder has suggested that a Chamber of Regions in the European parliament would be one desirable innovation. The whole idea of regional government could thus very well spring to life, with culturally and historically separate areas such as Scotland, Wales and (in the event of the entry of Spain to the EEC) the Basque country and Catalonia soon looking directly to Brussels over the shoulders of the old centres of government such as London, Paris or Madrid. Mr Michael Stewart's suggestions for direct elections to a European parliament have this beneficial direct consequence of creating a political substance for European regions immediately.

The English Labour movement has been a severely centralizing one, in many respects. For example, it has never explored whether a national wage level, imposed on the whole nation, thwarts the creation of employment in poor regions, just as large firms have been unenthusiastic about placing subsidiary branches in those same areas. Britain has anyway a more centralized political structure than have, in different ways, Italy or Germany, to its likely disadvantage in coming years.

There is another important point with which it is necessary to cope. In the old Europe of the Six, it was frequently suggested that the central areas were more prosperous than the remoter ones along the periphery, and Professor Kaldor, among others, has suggested that this process may continue once Britain is within the Community, causing us to become a kind of superior Sicily of the north. In fact, however, the original idea does not hold water. There are several central areas in the European Community which are quite depressed, such as Wallonia, Lorraine or the northern Ruhr or the German Eifel region; and many peripheral areas such as Marseilles and Bavaria which are well off. If the worst came to the worst, and for economic, psychological, or other reasons, Britain were indeed to become a real sick man of Europe, a new Southern Italy, it would surely be better for her to be inside the European Community rather than outside where nobody would be likely to bother about her fate at all. Still, the argument does not hold water in the first place.

The widespread popularity of the extremely ambiguous 'centre-periphery' hypothesis is surprising. An explanation may be found in its occurrence as one of the main conceptual themes in the social sciences. The hypothesis postulates a distinct geographic pattern within any economic and monetary union, comprising an 'advanced' centre and a 'backward' periphery, with flows of capital resulting in an accentuation of regional imbalances. It omits consideration of such countries as the USA, or Spain, or even nineteenth-century Germany, since those countries were politically united before the beginning of industrialization; though it might justifiably be pointed out that the economic advance of the US East coast and of California, of Catalonia and the Basque country, or of the Rhineland, would have occurred, even if there had been no prior political union.

The hypothesis has been formulated on a worldwide scale. But it is held as likely to apply at different geographical levels, and, specifically, at that of the European Economic Community. So far as Europe was concerned, the idea was expressed, for the first time, in 1955, by the UN Economic Commission for Europe, which decided that 'the countries situated near the economic centre of Europe are, in general, richer and more developed than those on the periphery'; and that 'the levels of economic development tend to be lowest in the regions furthest removed from the relatively small areas which developed as the main European centre of industrial activity, embracing England and the valley and outlet of the Rhine'. These views helped to establish the idea of a central Rhine axis, a revived Lotharingia, or a 'golden triangle'. The existence of a central Lotharingian axis, extending from Europort to Genoa, can indeed be shown by a simplified cartographical representation of such indices as population, industrial output per capita, electricity consumption per capita and so on. Such a representation seems to have an added significance because of the apparent concentration of development areas, and development zones, around the periphery of Western Europe.

But an analysis of this type is, however, superficial, a fact which becomes clear if statistics are examined for sub-regions. Such statistics, though as crude as those mentioned, in respect of regions in general, show both regions of under-development (such as the Rhineland-Palatinate) and regions of structural decline and depression (such as Lorraine) in the very heart of the so-called golden triangle. There are also many golden areas on the periphery of the European Community. Further, any careful study of the main economic sectors within the regions would soon dispel such a crude and 'total' explanation of prosperity or poverty as is posed by the centre-periphery hypothesis.

These criticisms have, it is true, been met after a fashion by the distinguished economist, Colin Clark, who has formulated a more sophisticated explanation of the dynamics of these problems. His theory was based on the determination of transport costs between the hundred or so regions of Western Europe. The economic potential of different regions is then assessed, and shown in aggregate form on maps which take into account extra-European trade and such tariffs as exist, since the area covered extends beyond the Community. His conclusion does point to a greater economic potential in the centre, with the Benelux area changing from being a place of relatively low economic potential to a high one after the entry of Britain and the other new members are taken into account.

But the study falls down when it attempts to correlate employment in expanding industries with areas of high economic potential during the periods 1950–60 (i.e. pre-EEC) and 1960–65 (the EEC era). No significant patterns emerge. Indeed, a general inspection of regional data on employment, migration and income fails to support the theory that expansion is related to a mystical 'central area'. Colin Clark's theory may also be questioned because of the reliance that it places, like other centre-periphery models, on transport costs. Such an emphasis seems unwarranted.

The question of centre-periphery effects is linked with that of monetary and economic union. But, in fact, the real regional problems of this adventure will be the economic consequences in particular fields, of which the most critical is likely to be the inability to devalue in the face of long-term differences in the regional rates of inflation.

8 Monopolies

There are several other anxieties about joining the Community, some major, some minor, which relate primarily to the economy. It has thus been suggested that the Common Market will 'mean takeovers and stronger monopolies', not to speak of 'vicious rationalization'. These remarks were made at Labour's Common Market conference, and they come curiously from a member of a party whose chairman was shortly to become Anthony Wedgwood Benn, whose enthusiasm, as Minister of Technology, for rationalizing mergers when in power was boundless, though he would no doubt say that he was concerned with national mergers within a single state.

There is no evidence that the European Community favours mergers any more than all modern, successful, and modernizing, political entities. Some of the European mergers that have occurred will help to close the gap between the size of US and European companies. A European Monopolies Commission as such is however desirable, extending beyond what is now done by the Commission. But something has been already done in these respects: and some examples may be recalled of the Commission's role in the control of monopoly: thus, in 1969, a case (with a fine of $490,000) was begun against ten chemical producers (including firms such as ICI and three Swiss firms which were not part of the EEC) for monopoly in the dyestuffs market, and action was also taken against quinine producers, against a cartel of ceramic tile manufacturers, against steel pipe producers, and so on. By the end of 1970, five inter-firm agreements were banned by the Commission, thirty-six abandoned by the firms themselves, and 589 adapted to meet its requirements. The Commission has also for example decided that Europemballage, a Brussels subsidiary of the American Continental Can Company, has abused its dominant position by trying to take over 80 per cent of the Dutch packaging company of Thomassen and Drijner-Verblifa, thus securing a virtual monopoly in northern Europe. Europemballage was told to dispose of this in July 1972. This sort of judgement has preoccupied the Commission in recent years, understandably, since mergers, agreements, or what Monsieur Mandel refers to as 'international interpenetration' has characterized economic developments since 1958.

On the other hand, the Commission has little power to prevent excessive investments in particular industries – for example, in steel. It would be desirable if it were able to take to its own the British law on the subject, whereby public interest, rather than damage to the market, became the criterion. British law prohibits, after all, any merger where the consequence would be to create an undertaking exceeding either £5M or $33\frac{1}{3}$ per cent of supply. In the meantime, on the continent, mergers on a vast scale have occurred – for example, the achievement of Ruhrkohle AG, a partly government-backed consortium of some twenty collieries producing about half what is mined by the National Coal Board. The Dunlop-Pirelli tyres merger is another example, in manufacturing, as is, in banking, the combination in 1971 of Credit Lyonnais, the Commerzbank and the Banco di Roma, to make the largest banking organization in Europe. In June 1972 Philips of Holland took complete control of Industrie Riunite Electrodomestici (IRE), Italy's largest refrigerator manufacturer, and a firm whose success was the most typical of those which did so well during the era of Italy's economic miracle. These actions and innumerable other actions similar, have created problems as yet unresolved by the Commission. But, if the Commission has not coped with them, how much more difficult would it be for single countries to do so? This is not to say that, as yet, Socialism, either in England or on the continent, has evolved the right answer to these colossal institutions; any more perhaps than it has evolved answers to the problems of civil services or of nationalized industries. But it must stand to reason, surely, that no answer is likely to be effective unless multinationally posed.

Similar problems arise from the fact that several advanced technological undertakings exist, in several European states, which are kept going either for prestige or for security reasons by the countries concerned. Such undertakings have been sometimes supported simply because governments have feared to hand over control of such matters to other countries or firms in other countries. That in itself is a strong argument for a European power structure, which will enable us to avoid such stupidities. Some excellent suggestions for creative undertakings along these lines have been brought together by Christopher Layton in his essay on 'Technology and Industry' in Richard Mayne's symposium, *Europe Tomorrow* : in particular, a European technological specialized agency, a European Science Foundation, and other special bodies similar to the Centre Européen de Recherches Nucléaires (CERN).

9 Transport and Energy

Another topic which has been greatly touched upon several times in the preceding argument without proper attention is transport. It seemed as if the differences between British and continental practices made it one of the areas where Britain could have considerable difficulty in the future. The problems and the real challenges are, however, common to all.

Transport obviously connects with questions of regional and urban planning. The future of cities, the prevention of the disintergration of their hearts in the style of the US, the control of crime, and the control of political alienation and political gangsterism, depend almost more on an effective transport policy than anything else. It is worthwhile noting the exemplary effects of the projects being developed in the declining northern Ruhr region. This has three designs: to prevent urban and social decentralization; to provide an efficient public transport; and to link the poor north of the Ruhr with the rich south. This has consequences, too, for the environment – as, indeed, transport policy does generally. Such questions as the new proposed axle weight of lorries cannot be regarded exclusively from the angle of economic priorities; while the fact that this subject has been discussed earlier, makes the point that transport is at the heart of modern political planning. This has become the century of the private car, more than of the common man. How many deaths and how much misery would have been avoided, how many homes and cities saved, if the social thinkers or the revolutionary writers of the generation of 1900 had concentrated their efforts upon this major threat to the old civilization, rather than upon fanciful general theories. It would be comforting to feel that had socialism come to power in Europe in 1910 rather than 1920, both wars and cars would have been avoided: but it is likely that the latter would anyway have been as uncontrollable as the first. Today, however, it may not be too late. The ephemeral or obsolescent character of the motor car gives ground for hope. The probability is that some collective policy without loss of personal freedom will be easier to reach within the Community than without. Whether it will is another matter.

The systems of transport in the Continental countries have grown up on the basis of national preoccupations and, in many cases, strategic ones. The needs of the nation states were served, not of the continent. A cheap, modern and well-organized transport system would be a great boon to Europe, in order to serve the commercial and other demands of the future. But, despite a European Conference of Transport Ministers, founded in 1953, and a permanent secretariat, little has been done. The Treaty of Rome obliges the EEC to seek a common transport policy, and several serious efforts have been made to put this into effect. But, partly because of a failure of political will (and French reluctance), partly because technological advance has moved quicker than anyone supposed probable (particularly in respect of private cars), the efforts were not fast enough. General principles were evolved in the Schaus memorandum in 1961, and an 'action programme' was produced in 1962. Arguments have continued over rates, licensing and quotas. Not much more has been done. This was fortunate for Britain, who might otherwise have found herself, after joining the Community, faced with attachment to an already sophisticated and complete network of air, rail, water and road paths. Transport too has been affected, obviously, and decisively, by such things as the transformation of Bavaria into an industrial region of the first importance, and the development of cities of pleasure, like those along the Mediterranean and Adriatic, and of the package tour.

With these developments, Britain has already been involved, to some extent. The continent, particularly Spain, but also

Germany and Italy, is now an essential part of the lives of many English people. Seven million British citizens travel to the continent every year for holidays. For that reason alone, a common transport policy would be desirable. The increasing amount of British goods which are sold on the continent also would obviously benefit immensely from common planning. Rail freight often adds 25 per cent to the prices of agricultural products. Common policies would reduce costs, increase the possibility of application of technology, and transform civic, as well as long distance, systems of communication. They would make possible the financing of otherwise uneconomic roads in backward regions (for example, Ireland) and effective planning would be able more easily to avoid excessive centralization and huge bottlenecks around terminals. In the cities such apparent dreams as Mrs Castle's single unit taxis or transcontinental, compressed-air pipelines might be more quickly possible. Common policies on aircraft safety, against hijackers or banditry, are obviously needed internationally.

A common energy policy would have similar beneficial circumstances. Once again, little enough has been done – and once again to British advantage, though much has been written. Coal was the responsibility of the old ECSC, oil, gas and electricity of the EEC. Coal has declined as the main source of energy since the formation of the ECSC and, in consequence, questions of a common policy have seemed less important than that of how to deal with the severe regional unemployment problems. Then the EEC's energy policy was closely related to the foreign policy, because of the increasing necessity to import oil. This, in its turn, has affected questions such as to whether or not to close coal mines temporarily uneconomic. The crux of this matter is, of course, that the energy problems of Western Europe link directly the advanced with the underdeveloped world. This postulates a continuous dialogue, in which the two societies whose needs are so different but severally seem so urgent, are forced into an alliance.

10 Taxation

Political writers spend a great deal of time discussing how money should be spent: 'the language of socialism is the language of priorities', Aneurin Bevan remarked once, in a rather over-quoted phrase. The question of how the money is to be raised receives less attention than it should. The Labour movement fought the general elections of 1959 specifically, and implicitly of 1964, 1966 and 1970, on the assumption that better labour relations, and more rational economic planning, would auto-matically increase revenue without increasing taxation. The question of whether or not common policies, such as have been suggested are desirable and necessary for transport and for energy, can be carried out, even if formulated, depends upon taxation and other revenues.

As in respect of labour, there are still several inhibitions on the continent preventing an absolutely free flow of capital. Some derive from exchange rates, some from taxation (such as double taxation of securities). Varying rates of taxation, on profits particularly, obviously inhibit freedom of capital movements. Therefore, the harmonization of taxation will be a major issue, and it will be essential to know what we want from this to ensure that our point of view is accepted.

The European Community has set out to harmonize the systems of taxation of the countries members of it, with the overt aim of removing 'distortions and barriers to investment' within the Community; and undoubtedly the implicit purpose is to reinforce political unification in yet one more material way. Many, however, such as Mr Douglas Jay, have criticized the

Community from the point of view that a 'major switch would . . . be made in the burden of taxation away from surtax and high incomes and profit-taxation, and on to food taxes and taxes on the main necessities of life'. Mr Jay naturally made a particular complaint about VAT, a general sales tax.

Here, undoubtedly, some critical points have to be considered: will redistributive taxation, for social purposes, be less possible? Are we not, perhaps, joining a club of tax evaders, since it is believed that one third of taxes are evaded in France, a half in Italy? Common fiscal policies are, however, ultimately essential to achieve the positive policies earlier described as desirable. Harmonization of indirect taxation is obviously necessary to secure the long term effects from the internification of competition. VAT is only one tax: income tax and profit tax, for example, remain. It will too be up to the British to insist upon the gradual adoption both of their aims in personal taxation and upon their ethics in matters of tax payments. It is true that the use of national taxation for social redistribution could be less easy after Britain joins the Community, but it also is possible that the co-ordination of fiscal policies called for by Articles 2 and 104 of the Treaty of Rome could be worked to our advantage. A side aspect of the adoption of a common fiscal policy would be the possibility of a reduction of tax havens for the rich and tax-evading companies – in, for example, the Channel Islands, Monaco, Liechtenstein and Switzerland. These things are likely to be only possible as a result of real international pressure.

Does the Value Added Tax really 'shift the burden of taxation from the wealthy to the low paid' as Reg Bottini put it at the Labour Party conference in 1970? Certainly, VAT, a very broad based tax with few exceptions, constitutes a fiscal revolution. In one sense, too, all indirect taxation is more regressive than direct, since it is in the nature of a poll tax, and makes no distinction between the different circumstances of those who pay it. This applies to purchase tax, SET and so on, as much as to VAT. Purchase tax attempted to tax 'luxuries', but, by now, the definition of that has become difficult. As Vic

Feather suggested at the Trade Union Conference in 1970, it would be possible, even essential, to arrange that the less well-off could be given safeguards to counter the effects of VAT. VAT, at the moment, does not affect either food or the building of houses, and there are some other exceptions. It is, of course, a flexible tax, able to be levied on difficult sections of the economy and on different products. Sweden has already adopted VAT, independent of the Community, and the Conservative government has said that it would have brought in this tax anyway. It was certainly one of the favourite reforms advocated by Iain Macleod when in opposition. Finland and Austria, outside the Community, are going to introduce this tax, and it is also being examined in the US and in Japan. The probability is that VAT will become the standard form of indirect taxation in the Western world. The attraction from a social point of view is that it makes no distinction for any person when he is spending money on goods and services as to what he will buy. The disagreeable thing, of course, is that it makes no difference between essentials, which the poor have to have anyway, and the luxuries which they could never afford. VAT could, however, be used as a regulator, just as purchase tax was, and VAT abolishes SET as well as purchase tax. It also prevents tax evasion. So far as the European Community is concerned, the point of VAT is that it is a tax neutral at national borders as it is in other respects. It enables a tax on an item which is exported to be identified exactly, and re-dated on export. It is responsible for 10–15 per cent of the member countries' revenues. In general, the tax is levied at a higher rate in most of the Community countries than it is in Britain at the moment, and the system differs slightly in the Community from what the Conservatives plan for Britain. A disadvantage is that it is complicated to administer, both for businessmen and tax collectors. Whereas seventy thousand persons are registered in Britain for purchase tax, there will be about one and a half million for VAT. Further zero ratings, such as are urged by the theatrical profession and other affected groups, could well be introduced, but only provided the rate was raised say to $12\frac{1}{2}$ per cent.

The abolition of the distinction between luxuries and essentials, implicit in the transferral from purchase tax to VAT, may also be in the long run unpracticable. It seems rather unlikely, for example, that the mass production of irrelevant consumer goods will be able to continue indefinitely even in advanced countries. Looking far ahead, the acceptance of a tighter personal regime in all sorts of ways is almost certain to be a condition of continuing political liberty. Education, washing machines, a varied diet, the preservation of the countryside, and of a free press – these things are not luxuries; but more than one motor car is since it uses up the community's space and air and should be liable, in future, to be taxed as such. The essential criterion should be the effect of the alleged 'unnecessary' spending of the community's resources: there are many 'luxuries' which may be luxurious by old standards, but they have no deleterious consequences for the communities resources. These things can simply be taxed at the standard VAT rate. A gold-plated Daimler, in the style of Lady Docker, or gold taps with hammers and sickles instead of hot and cold, as one famous English socialist insisted upon for his bathroom, uses up a scarce resource which the community needs. At all events, despite the abolition of purchase tax, we must expect in future that society will want to tax socially useless luxuries in a different way from essentials. The task of deciding which is which will naturally demand flexibility, humanity and vision and these decisions will undoubtedly be reached better on a European or international level than a narrow national one in the light of the general availability of resources.

11 Growth and Environment

A further argument to place against the suggestion that British entry into Europe would increase the pace of our economic growth is that the whole idea of growth has become discredited. This is a powerful point to make. Nevertheless, it would seem likely that, only on an international, or at least a European, basis can the problems attendant on uncontrolled growth be resolved; it stands to reason that there are questions, such as pollution in international waterways like the Danube or the Rhine, oil wastes from shipwrecked tankers, aviation noise, which can only be internationally resolved. But the same is true of many less obvious problems. The European Commission has made as constructive an approach to these problems as has been attempted by anyone else.

The reader of newspapers and journals in 1972 has been veritably deluged with information and arguments, on these subjects, so much so that it is difficult to be certain what to think. Are we really running out of essential commodities, or using up 'more than our fair share?' Has population growth really reached an intolerable level? What is threatened more, the old countryside or the old streets? Is noise or smell really a threat to health? And so on. Every political party has paid lip service to these ideas and for the first time a little seems to be being done, though the essentially moral questions at stake have not been satisfactorily resolved. The fact is that economic growth cannot simply be disdained, since only by that means can the riches be created which will make possible social advances. That is particularly true of Britain, whose rate of growth is so slow.

Whether we like it or not, low growth remains the reason for the lack of British competitiveness in international markets. The same is even more true of countries of the Third World who can only look to economic growth to assist their rise out of primary misery. A global restriction on growth by governmental or inter-governmental action would help to maintain the existing unequal *status quo* between nations and social groups.

Furthermore, while human nature may well be using up one variety of resources, human ingenuity, and improvization, are such that it is impossible to believe this is as serious a problem as doomsters have suggested: has there ever been a time when human beings have known for certain that they had as many as fifty years' supply of a given material?

Of all the various problems, that of population growth seems likely to be the most demanding in the future. But the difficulties will scarcely be encountered in any of the countries of the European Community, with their low rate of population growth and their inexhaustible need for more labour. The problems will be major ones wherever the rate of population growth is greater than about 2 per cent a year, and great in places such as Mexico where the figure is higher. In Europe, even so, the antisocial misuse of land, air and water can, and should, be severely taxed. In Europe too, general policy on environmental questions demand, as elsewhere, large-scale analysis affecting the whole social development, including transport, housing and other services of an area or a quarter. In some respects, this argument naturally dovetails into a consideration of regional policies.

European countries can certainly learn much from each other: the problems between town and country, of new towns, of cities with old dying hearts, shipwrecked oil tankers, the problems of noise from aircraft – all these are multinational problems. We can all learn a good deal too from for example the imaginative schemes under discussion in the northern part of the Ruhr.

The recent proposals of Dr Mansholt, the present President

of the European Commission, seem too to have much to commend them: he has suggested that Gross National Product as an idea should be replaced by that of Gross National Utility – thus plainly suggesting heavy taxes on, or even prohibitions upon, the manufacture of socially useless products. He went on to suggest a system whereby products should be made clean and recycled against pollution, and then would secure certain certificates; the VAT would be altered to favour these; special extra taxes would be levied on imports which had not been properly treated, so encouraging the USA and, perhaps, the Soviet *bloc* within a few years to adopt the same system; and special grants to the Third World would be made to assist with their own recycling (though this is easier said than done). Dr Mansholt has also suggested promotion, by fiscal and other means, of the durability of consumer goods: new cars might pay 100 per cent tax, cars which are five years old would pay 50 per cent, and still older cars would pay nothing. (Sweden, though outside the EEC, already builds cars to last.) Dr Mansholt concluded: 'The problems raised by non-polluting production based on recycling still represent a huge unexplored field. Until now, research has been almost entirely devoted to growth. We must divert it towards "utility", towards "well-being". An evident solution would be to end the ever-lasting drama of the Euratom research budget and to transform it into a research programme directed exclusively towards [these] objectives.' All economists who have been in any way concerned with this subject have explained that the reason why there is a pollution problem is that the environment does not carry a price representing its correct social scarcity value. If those who caused pollution were made to pay for it, that in itself would lead to an informed use of scarce resources.

These ideas may not be the perfect solution to all the problems concerned. The suggestion for the Third World may not be a practicable one. Nor are they particularly original: it was Monsieur Robert Poujade who first used the phrase 'Make the polluters pay!' But they are intelligent, and quite inspiring proposals, demanding the intervention of the Community, in the general, long-term interests of the people of Europe – and of the rest of the world. Dr Mansholt prefaced this argument, incidentally, with the declaration that the US at the moment did not 'possess the necessary political strength for the solution of its major problems'.

The problem in England is complicated by the current pressure on land, the shortage of houses, the consequent increase in housing prices, the ambiguity of powers of authorities, the Conservative party's obsession with dogma (for example, the Housing Finance Act) and the general crisis in local authority housing. It is evident, too, that, within the Community, Dr Mansholt's ideas have not everywhere found favour: his excellent speech was specifically attacked by the French communist party, as by Monsieur Raymond Barre, his own vice-president. This should not disguise the fact that a British presence, in the Community centres of decision, is the only way for us to attempt to control the situation.

The long-term solution to these questions also necessitates a more vigorous approach to population questions. Here again, the collaboration of Britain in a larger unit than that of these islands, would presumably assist our, and the world's, pursuit of the stabilization of population – even if, to be practical, this may only be achieved at a basis of twice our world's present level, or at approximately 7,000 million,* a figure which will almost certainly be reached by the year 2000. (7,000 million may seem too high a figure for decent stabilization; but let us be optimistic, since it is improbable that the population of the world will be less than that in twenty-five years time.) Population reduction is also not quite inconceivable.

Dr Mansholt has also, it is worthwhile pointing out, a refreshingly original attitude towards most of the problems connected with growth of population, and the problems of the city. It was a relief, comforting in itself, to find so humane and experimental a socialist at the head, even if only temporarily, of such a modern institution as the European Commission. Is there any other prominent European politician other than Dr

* 7 US billion.

Mansholt who speaks, and realistically, in the manner of William Morris? In place of Rolls-Royce and Fiats, Mr Mansholt foresees free buses and trains. In place of 'cages on 42nd floors', he foresees men working outside cities altogether. In place of vast factories, he sees men working in groups of, say, twenty and controlling their own work. No one would be allowed to make a car that lasted only five years. Repair would become normal, new the exception. Dr Mansholt added thoughts about a three-day week, and how he expected that, though people would become less materially rich, they would be better educated, and 'would like pleasant things like music' and be happier in their more congenial work. The fact that, in the second half of the twentieth century, a man such as Dr Sicco Mansholt can capture the position of Presidency of the Commission is itself a matter of the greatest encouragement.

A long-term approach to environmental questions also raises the question of land and its ownership. As Professor Phlipponneau pointed out recently, authoritarian socialist politics, as practised in Eastern Europe, has the all important advantage of the complete public ownership of land: 'it makes it easy to respect the historic character of urban centres, and even to restore them at whatever price, after total destruction ... the absence of all speculation in real property helps town planning conservation and the establishment of open spaces. ... A cheap and well-organized system of public transport makes it possible to separate residential and working areas.'[39] This situation has, indeed, preserved Eastern Europe, and much of the Soviet world generally, from the blight of development. The so-called revolutionary countries have been far better at conservation than have the West, and the loving care with which the Poles have reconstructed Breslau/Wroclaw, or with which the Communist officials show the visitor the palaces of Moscow, Budapest (or Havana) is a touching commentary on the love for tradition that lurks close beneath the revolutionary skin. Golo Mann, a few years ago, pointed out, in the *New York Review of Books*, how the spirit of the still semi-pastoral Germany of his youth could be far more easily recaptured in the communist East than in the abrasive West of Germany. But this preservation has been done at a cost most Western Socialists would rightly regard as unacceptable. The nationalization of development land has been proposed in the recent Labour party draft manifesto to defeat speculation, and help the housing situation. But it is most improbable that it will ever be put into effect, if only because the cost of compensation at current prices would be an astronomic burden on the taxes. Communist behaviour in their cities is too the direct obverse of that of the Japanese in theirs: in the one, static attitudes, in the other, excessive dynamism, have preserved housing shortages, created slums, and left insanitary and polluted atmospheres in factories. Meantime, as Professor Sasse has put it, 'large sectors of the population are not so much directed at a mere increase of their individual prosperity, as to socio-political revision of the overall system: their claims for a more equitable distribution of income, improved public services ... improvement of human environment, humanization of industrial work, and "participation", begin to dominate the domestic political scene'. In a word, in the 1970s, aesthetics has re-entered politics – and, none too soon.

12 Agriculture

The question of land obviously brings up the question of agriculture. First, it is improbable that British membership of the EEC will much affect employment in agriculture. In 1960, 20 per cent of the working population of the original Six (about 15 million people) worked on the land, either as labourers or as farmers: by 1972, only 14 per cent (under 10 million); and, by 1980, in consequence of the Mansholt Plan (described below), and of old age, there will probably be only 7 per cent (half of the agricultural labour force of the old EEC was over fifty). This reduction is almost unequalled in agricultural history, except in Russia under Stalin. But Britain has today a bare 3 per cent of its working population living on the land. Bearing in mind the larger expanse of land on the continent, it is doubtful if there is much difference between the level of farm employment already reached in this country, and that which will probably be reached on the continent by 1980. Most English farms are of a size likely to be viable in the Community. Britain has devoted a larger sum to agricultural research than have European countries. The level of yield in Britain compares very well with that prevalent on the continent. (The average eggs per hen for example in the UK is 206, in France only 147; wheat production per hectare in the 1960s averaged 4,000 kilos in the UK, 3,000 kilos in France and only a little over 2,000 in Italy.) In normal conditions, except in special circumstances in the agricultural economy (such as small-scale chicken farmers, vegetable and apple growers, also glass-house producers), British agriculture should prosper in the

EEC. In general, big farmers will do best, and small farmers the least well; as is the case in the Community at the moment.

For, from the start, agriculture in the EEC was allowed a separate status. This was primarily because, in the late 1950s, at the time of the inception of the Community, two-thirds of the farms in the whole market were of less than twenty-five acres. Full free trade from the beginning in agricultural products would have given great advantages to the more efficient, larger farmers, and would have created social injustices, and also political difficulties, for both the French and the German regimes of the time. The Treaty of Rome therefore, instructed the Commission to work out a policy to ensure that, despite social problems and political difficulties, farming would receive a 'fair return approaching those in other sectors of the economy', a policy which, as the Commission was frank enough to admit, would mean that prices in the Community could not be at the same level as those on the world market, but would be 'stabilized' at a higher level. Target Community prices were fixed, variable levies on imported goods imposed, in place of the usual customs duties, to make the price of the imported goods the same as the domestic price. In addition, there is official 'support buying' to take off the market any excess of supply over demand at the price level. Out of a total Community Budget of £1,670M, 95 per cent goes on farm support (of which only a fraction to help modernize farm buildings).

No one is happy with the present system. Even farmers have been angry. It seems lop-sided, it has inadequate means of reform, and gives little consideration to environmental and amenity questions. Food surpluses (particularly in wheat, butter and the always politically complex product, sugar) have grown – Europe's 'mountain of butter' once having been 300,000 tons. There is still a gap between agricultural and industrial incomes. Rich, not poor, families have chiefly benefited. Many of the latter are still poor, and believe themselves disgracefully underpaid for their products. Breton farmers have poured hundreds of gallons of milk into rivers and ditches in protest at the prices they receive. The financing of the arrangements (import levies ensure that importing countries pay the most) have imposed an unequal burden on member states in relation to benefits. Thus, Britain, the largest food importer in the world, will pay nearly 19 per cent of the European Community's costs, in return for 6 to 7 per cent of benefits. There has been an undoubtedly bad effect on world trade, both in respect of other agricultural producers like the US and of other developing countries. An enquiry into prices received by farmers in the Community, Britain and the USA, made it clear that the CAP has been manipulated to ensure a high level of prices for the farmers of the continent. This has prevented the ordinary public of the Community from buying food at low prices, and the low cost food producers of the world from gaining access to the European market.

Industry has been specially critical of the CAP, British industry included: Michael Clapham, who became president of the Confederation of British Industry in 1972, chose to devote his first speech as president to attack the CAP, commenting, a little superciliously perhaps, that the CAP was a solution to a problem that 'we had solved a century ago'. British industry, therefore, will probably be among the strongest proponents of change once the country is in a position to be effective on this matter.

The revisions which were proposed in the CAP by the Mansholt Plan (or 'Agriculture 1980', as it was technically known), would resolve some of these problems. The Council of Ministers, in March 1972, accepted some of this plan's suggestions – introducing interest-free rebates on taxes to allow for modernization; pensions (of $600 for a single man and $900 for a couple) to retired farmers; and increased retraining facilities for those leaving the land. But the Council did not accept in full the central idea of the Mansholt plan, the 'economically viable farm' – defined as one where farmers kept accounts, were professionally able, and had a development plan, enabling it, within six years, to give two full-time workers an income of $10,000 to $12,500 a year, and would not need more than 2,300 hours of work per man. The Council's reticence was, as usual, due to political hostility. Mansholt's successor, as the member of the Commission responsible for agriculture, Carlo Scarascia Mugnozza, has, however, also publicly backed a revision of agricultural policies; in his first press conference, in June 1972, he explained his belief that 'the old emphasis in high prices as the principal means of supporting farmers should give way to a greater emphasis on structural reforms – measures to promote rationalization, modernization and investment'.

Still, despite shortcomings, the CAP was a remarkable political achievement. It achieved a managed continent-wide market for most agricultural products within the Community, and better security for most of her farmers. National systems of price support have been abolished. A vast amount of work has been done in an attempt to reach fair prices for most commodities. It can even be looked upon as a socialist policy in principle, since after all it seeks to establish full control of market prices by a central body. Its aim is to help the poorest section of the community, by means of a transfer of income from the richer one. It derived, broadly, from the national policies of the countries of the old EEC before 1958. Everyone admits the defects of the present CAP and, within the EEC, as Frank Sykes has pointed out in an interesting article in *Country Life* in 1972, 'we shall find ourselves for the first time for more than a century belonging to a society with a significant agricultural lobby'.[40] It should also be borne in mind that Britain's own system for farmers involves subsidies considerably higher than in the EEC, while, over the last ten years, a policy of import control has been followed in Britain too. Though the system is different from that of the Community, it has had a similar protective aim. The difference was that Britain and the continent have, for historical and economic reasons, for many generations followed, in general, quite different policies from Britain, of importing cheap food from the Empire, and compensating farmers at home. One reason for not operating a British system was the size of the tax burden that would have been involved. As Donald Swann sagely pointed out: 'This burden is largely psychological. Consumers in the Six pay taxes which are lower than they would be if a deficiency payments system existed, but, of course, they pay higher market prices for food than would exist under a deficiency payments scheme.'

What will happen in Britain now is quite easy to predict. English wheat, for instance, will rise in value 'at the farm gate' (about £10). Wheat production will, probably, therefore, also rise, with consequences for English bread, until now primarily made from Canadian hard wheat. Barley, for cattle feed, will rise similarly in value, somewhat less because of the recent development of a new maize in France with higher yield. More probable is an expansion in beef and mutton, whose price is likely to rise considerably, and in mixed farming. Acres under grass are likely to increase once Britain is fully within the market. The 'beef crisis' in the middle of 1972 was, doubtless, a short term one, but it indicated how farmers can hope to prosper in this respect, once Britain (and Ireland) is within the Community. It is possible that, in consequence, the high percentage (about 80 per cent) of supply to the British market will drop somewhat, but before alarmists go further in wondering about the collapse of the roast beef of old England, they should remember that, before the war, British farms produced only about half of the beef eaten here. (Argentina, our chief supplier in the 'good old days', has been unable to produce enough to meet her own supplies: in Buenos Aires, in 1971, there was even a beefless week.)

Sugar beet, milk production, and pig and poultry farming, will not be greatly affected, and the trend towards industrialized production of the latter is likely to increase: it would increase anyway. Perhaps English bacon farmers will be able to win back some of the trade from the Danes, our EFTA rivals. Potatoes are already produced here in too great numbers, so that the acreage will decrease there – to the certain profit of the distended English stomach. Vegetables grown to be tinned or otherwise processed will surely increase, the business being already in the hands of large firms.

One problem to be faced by English agriculture from the Common Market is marketing. As a direct consequence of a less highly capitalized agricultural sector, continental methods are more expert and on a larger scale than ours, though, as Frank Sykes put it, 'they are faced with the troubles inherent in such organization, of having to please everyone'. Still, probably only the English Milk Marketing Board is quite up to Community methods.

It is also possible that, within a few years at most, the EEC will insist that Britain extend the VAT to food. Already, from April 1973, it seems, certain items which, for the moment, are curiously regarded as not food (ice cream, potato crisps, salted nuts, chocolate biscuits, fruit juices, syrups) will be taxed at the full VAT rate. In future, normal food will probably be covered, unless Britain wishes to delay matters on a considerable scale, in the manner of Italy.

Meantime, there will be another effect upon the European Community itself: the British market will be very helpful indeed to the CAP. As John Marsh and Pierre Uri have put it, in Richard Mayne's *Europe Tomorrow*, the British import levies and the availability of the British market 'will restore the CAP to solvency. Surplus pressures will be reduced, and the need for subsidized exports will disappear.'

In general, Britain should press for a reform of the CAP from the moment we are in the Community. One sensible alternative scheme has been proposed by Christopher Ritson and John Marsh, lecturers at the University of Reading in that university's department of agricultural economics, in their pamphlet, *Agricultural Policy and the Common Market*. In brief, this idea assumes that the best approach would be to lower the prices of surplus commodities. That, in its turn, would demand that direct payments be made to offset the reduction, and paid to the poorer sections of the agricultural community. Pensions, subsidies and compensation to those who moved out of agriculture would grow. The present practice of dumping surpluses would be brought to an end, and price rules would have to be strictly maintained, without fluctuation. The prices would take into account (if not necessarily follow in every respect) world prices, and have special relationships, if that phrase of old repute can now be used again, with such as sugar cane producers in tropical, or sub-tropical, countries. After all, as Marsh and Ritson point out, 'the Community has a vital interest in the health of world trade'. Its own prosperity is closely linked to the existence of a buoyant export market for manufactured goods.

These measures and, indeed, every wise or humane proposal for the modernization and rationalization of European industry, admittedly, have long-term social and aesthetic consequences. Depopulation of rural areas, modern farming methods, the creation of commerce and industry in areas hitherto reserved for agriculture, reafforestation, are all probable opportunities to be coped with or refused over the next generation.

Then it has been pointed out that continental deep sea fishing threatens ruin to parts of Scotland and to other places dependent on that trade. In fact, the Commission's fisheries policies have much to commend them from a Socialist point of view: as a variant to the now accepted six-mile limit, a twelve-mile limit has been agreed in areas where the nature of stocks and the dependence of the local population on fishing requires it. Britain retains full powers to stipulate methods of fishing – size of nets for example – up to twelve miles. There is also to be a comprehensive review of the whole question before any further change in 1982. The Commission has, finally, not only given critical aid to certain fishing industries but, in its guide price and withdrawal price, has fixed up a system similar to the CAP, in the interests of avoiding a fluctuation of prices.

Much of the argument over the EEC has concerned the cost of living; but costs are ultimately less important than standards, though, even if the argument were to be kept to that matter, prices of food have scarcely remained static outside the European Community. Indeed, prices in England have gone up faster than they have in the EEC itself (partly because world food prices have risen faster than European ones), and, we have, it should be recalled, a five years' period of transition before we feel the full impact. (In 1967 to 1970 we were being told that food prices, on entry into the Community, might increase by some 15 per cent. These figures were interpreted by some as being themselves grounds for not entering the Common Market. But such increases occur even outside the Community, and the Conservative minister of food had to admit that the price of food between June 1970 and June 1972 had gone up 17·4 per cent.)

Much has been said, persuasively, on the subject of cheap Commonwealth food, both by people using the argument to try and strengthen British ties with the Commonwealth *per se*, and those who think that it is more economical, as well as more virtuous, to buy food from the Commonwealth. But though the production of food from the underdeveloped world may very well go up, it may not continue to come so easily our way. One does not have to be a doomster on the subject of famine to believe that, even if famine is averted, the price of food will generally increase.

This affects the general discussion about the cost of food when Britain is within the Market. This is a part of the argument, indeed, where the anti-Marketeers have concentrated their fire: we are going, we are told, to have to abandon 'our 120-year-old policy of cheap food ... a switch of supply from traditional low cost suppliers to the high cost inefficient farms of Western Europe': thus Mr Peter Shore. 'A pound of sausages will take the place of the weekend joint.' Thus Diana Jeuda, the defeated Labour candidate in the Macclesfield by-election of 1971, adding, a trifle inconsequently, that butter will have to give way to margarine. The English sausage itself is held to be threatened, not to speak of the kipper – or, at least, its colour. British beer, we are also told, is in danger.* The English way of eating would be seriously, and, therefore, adversely affected. British bread would give way to French, and British purple sweets would give way to French scarlet ones. And

---

* This is an allusion to the occasion when the EEC wanted to allow the import of cheap beer, made from maize and rice, into Germany where the regulations only provided for barley-made beer. No attempt was made to alter German beer. Another question related to beer made from male and female hops.

all in order to achieve agricultural self-sufficiency within the expanded Europe of the Nine.

By these and other arguments, half emotive and allusive, and half economic, the anti-Marketeers within the Labour movement have created what seems, at first hearing, a powerful case; and, doubtless, had they achieved a referendum in this country on the issue of the Common Market, these arguments would have been developed even further; lurid pictures would have been conjured up of oily continental foods or sauerkraut being forcibly fed to protesting British housewives. In addition, while prices would be going up, Britain would have to contribute, to the Community's Agricultural Fund, a substantial and ominously undefined sum, perhaps £400M a year, perhaps even £600M, to prop up the incompetent husbandmen of Aquitaine, Apulia or Bavaria.

These are critical questions, to be sure; but they are separate questions. Our diet and our eating habits are not the same as their cost; and the first have been changing over the last few years, as it is, in some ways towards European customs, and in some, regrettable, ways towards American ones. (When the bakers proudly defended the 'English loaf' (sic) at their conference at Torquay in 1972, they omitted reference to the sliced loaf of the US, which is rather more often seen in modern supermarkets). But our diet has, in the home, anyway, remained remarkably static for the last twenty years. Many, perhaps most, would say that a change towards continental standards of food has much to commend it, from a dietary angle; and, indeed, from the angle of social equality, as well, there is much to be said. 'The price of butter' is given lip service as a yardstick by which to judge the difference between British and continental prices, but few trouble to point out that British salted butter is much less palatable than continental fresh butter. (The British variety is obsolete, dating from pre-refrigerator days.) In Britain, two things too stand out as the superficial, but distinctive, marks of class: the first is accent, the second food. A middle-class Englishman enters a working-class restaurant, or even a working-class home, to find the standard of consumption quite different from his own: and *vice versa*. The war of the two teas, China and Indian, is a characteristic campaign of the British class war. In these ways, continental countries are more egalitarian: French lorry drivers' cafés are so good as to have been for many years a gastronomic attraction.

There is a specific historical reason for this: the late Raymond Postgate explained, in his introduction to the *Good Food Guide* a few years ago, how the industrial revolution in Britain took so long, and began so long ago, that the British urban family has lost touch with the herbs and other country produce to which the French, Italians and Germans are more close. In consequence, it seems that, even in so personal a matter as food habits, association with the Community will assist equality. A Spanish anarchist recently described his experiences in prison in Teruel and described how bad the food was; he added 'Years later I tasted the food in a London factory canteen where English friends worked, at wages which would seem a fortune in Spain. The food was of so poor a standard, it would have started a riot in prison. Yet nobody complained. When I pointed it out to them, they laughed and agreed.'[41]

The question of the cost of food is a more complicated one. It is obvious that the shop price of food will increase, though precisely by how much is uncertain. To this it can be replied, first, that, as people grow richer, the proportion of their income that they spend upon food anyway decreases, so that, if our general wealth increases within the EEC, the proportion of our incomes to be spent on food will, within a few years, be less than it is now; second, that the price of food has anyway gone up and, as suggested earlier, the possibility of cheap food from the Commonwealth is unlikely to be a permanent characteristic for the rest of time. (For example, even in 1972, and before Britain joined the Community, the prices for New Zealand lamb have gone up sharply, suggesting that, as Godfrey Brown in the *Financial Times* put it, 'The signs are that New Zealand has had enough of shipping meat vast distances for such a low return'.)

Any detailed comparative study of consumer prices of any

sort leads to a great many surprising difficulties. The European Community, and the ILO both publish consumer price indexes designed to compare prices of items 'representative of the consumption patterns of the population concerned'. In deciding what is 'representative', there is room for many disputed judgements. The increase in prices in certain items will affect different classes in different ways. Nor are food and drink the only important items in most budgets and nor is an increase in the availability of food, consumer durables, housing, clothing and so on, necessarily uniform. Even within a single commodity there are no uniform criteria: there are more television sets and telephones in use per thousand people in Britain than there are in the European Community as a whole, and about the same number of cars. What, however, is certain is that the recent growth in spending upon all main items which go to make the tables of statistics has been greater in the Community than it has in Britain.

13 Economic Planning in Europe

The need for economic planning, both with regard to specific economic areas, such as transport or energy, as well as at a geographical level, through regional policy, has appeared as a major theme in the previous analysis.

Economic planning was viewed by many progressive people, especially in the mid–1960s, as a solution to all economic problems, particularly those of low economic growth and high inflation. Indeed, it was considered as an essential prerequisite in a modern, post-industrial society in which mixed enterprises played an important part.

The idea of economic planning common in the mid–1960s extended beyond regional interventions, or interventions in specific sectors of the economy, and embraced the whole of economic decision-making. This approach, championed by the Labour government between 1964–6, also sought to create a new economic mechanism, a system neither socialist nor capitalist in the traditional sense, but instead a unique combination of private enterprise decision-making at the so-called 'micro-level', and overall public guidance at the so-called 'macro-level'.

The idea inspiring, and largely adopted by, the Labour government was the French system of 'planification', originally devised by the 'father of European Unity', Jean Monnet. This system involved the formulation of five-year national plans including medium-targets for the main 'macro-economic' sectors – increase in GNP, price inflation, employment, foreign trade – as well as targets for specific 'micro-economic' sectors, such as the chemical or the engineering industries. The targets were not, like their Soviet counterparts, coercive, but purely 'indicative'. It was assumed that public enterprise would adopt them, resulting in a more efficient pattern of production. At the same time, the targets were placed deliberately high, on the optimistic assumption that that would increase the 'demand expectations' of private entrepreneurs, and induce them to invest more, thus boosting economic growth.

The element of optimism entailed in the assumption that 'indicative planning' would be a panacea for all economic problems, and create a new economic system, adapted to the view of the world put forward persuasively by J. K. Galbraith in *The New Industrial State*, contained a more ambitious ideal: that the process towards greater economic planning in the West would be parallelled by an obverse movement away from coercive planning in the East, entailing, as it did, a major problem of inefficiency and misallocation of resources, towards a technocratically determined and ideal world.

The notion of convergence seemed to be supported by events in all parts of Europe in the mid–1960s: Britain, and even Germany, were moving towards the French system of planification, as was Italy, which adopted its first National Plan in 1965. The whole nature of 'modern capitalism', oligopolistic and behaviourist, seeking security and recognizing 'social costs' and the need for planning, rather than *laissez-faire* and 'optimizing' in the search for profit, seemed to have undergone a change. The output of the public sector was in many countries exceeding 50 per cent of national output, and public interventions were proliferating.

In the East, Yugoslavia in 1965, and Hungary and Czechoslovakia in 1968, embarked upon major reforms, while even Russia seemed to be anticipating major changes in her limited reforms of 1965. Certainly, in the case of Yugoslavia, a decisive move was made towards the adoption of the profit motive, of market-determined prices, of greater enterprise decision-making and a participation in the international division of labour (while retaining public ownership). All this, it seemed to the Left, had been achieved within the context of the nation state. Indeed, any involvement in supranational integration would, it seemed, merely result in a compromise between those countries, willing, under socialist direction, to embrace the new economic philosophies, and those refusing to do so. As a consequence, little would be achieved by extending the area of operations; indeed, there might be a serious danger that existing achievements might be repealed.

By 1972, these last arguments had become meaningless, and the technocratic dream of a new economic system lay shattered.

In the West, even the French became increasingly disillusioned with planification. In part, the disillusionment was a specific complaint by the Left that the plans were undemocratic, and represented the interests of big business, although such a situation could presumably have been changed by a non-Gaullist government. More specifically, however, the targets themselves were seen to be inaccurate. Totally new and 'intermediate' plans had to be introduced. As a result, the Vth and VIth French plans witnessed considerable changes, attempting to introduce more flexibility and greater co-ordination, with short-term economic policy. In doing so, however, the original aim of the plan as an independent, medium-term instrument, central to economic strategy, was undermined.

In Britain, the devaluation of 1967 produced the collapse of the Department of Economic Affairs and George Brown's National Plan and, for a time at least, produced a reaction resulting in the return of *laissez-faire* capitalism with the Conservative government after June 1970. In Italy, too, major difficulties were involved in the fulfillment of the 1966–70 Plan.

In all these cases, the prime responsibility for the failure of the Plans lay in external circumstances, in particular the problems of internal inflation and the chronic balance of payments. This situation, common enough in Britian, was most markedly portrayed by the changing economic fortunes of France. Thus, during the 1950s, when France was still largely a 'closed' autocratic economy, the Plans worked relatively well. Once, with the removal of tariffs (a liberalization which, it should be noted, was *not* merely the result of membership of the Community, but represented a world-wide trend, supervised by GATT), the French economy became more open, similar to the British, payments problems set in, and the Plans of the late 1950s and early 1960s were upset.

The lessons for those members of the Labour party who see a 'socialist Britain' as an alternative to membership of the Community are clear: however desirable a well-planned, mixed economy Britain, let alone a purely socialist one, might be, the goal is quite impossible without a socialist Europe – the Europe with which, through our trading relationship, we are directly linked; indeed, through our increasing trade with Europe, this link is all the time growing.

How realistic is this venture? Already some, if limited, progress has been made in planning at the Community-level by the designation by the European Commission of three medium-term Economic Policy Programmes (MTEPP). The first MTEPP (1966–8) was agreed after strong opposition by the (then) Conservative government of West Germany, and represented a major conversion of the latter to the idea of economic planning – a conversion achieved, it should be said, through the Community process. In a similar way, the British Conservative government will have to accept the interventionist doctrine of the third MTEPP of 1972 onwards.*

To date, the MTEPP is vague and provides only broad, extrapolated targets, with no sectional break-down. However, the general climate within the Community is favourably disposed to the idea of greater intervention, not in the wildly optimistic way of the past, but viewing it as a major component of a complex economic structure.

The need for a European approach, and the failure of the search for a 'new economic mechanism', is also exhibited by the

---

* In the same context, it is interesting to note that the Commision has proposed an organ at the Community level akin to the IRC abolished by the Conservatives who would persumably be under pressure to accept participation in the project when it comes to fruition.

experience of Eastern Europe in the late 1960s. Russian reforms have been stifled, and the evil aftermath of the 'Prague Spring' is well known. In Hungary too, progress has been scant. Perhaps most significantly of all, Yugoslavia, which had become the model 'alternative' economic system of the moderate Left, now seems to have merely succeeded in substituting the classic symptoms of a socialist economy – lack of incentive, bureaucracy, irrational allocation of resources, taking little account of consumer demand – for those of the classic capitalist economy, such as mass unemployment, emigration, high inflation, and payments problems.

Any 'convergence' between the East and West of Europe cannot, therefore, be solved by the vain efforts of individual countries. It can be governed, on the one hand, by a redefinement of the economic systems, something only possible at the European level, and, on the other hand, by the political achievement of a lasting *detente*, which can only be achieved by a real European Security Conference and, as has already been shown, such a conference is more likely to succeed if a common stance is adopted by the countries of the European Community.

For these reasons, both realistic and idealistic, a European approach is essential. Any attempt to realize the alternative approach of socialism in one country is clearly doomed to failure, and will only benefit the reactionary elements in our society, and perpetuate existing inequalities.

14 The Alternatives

Speaking in 1971 about economic prospects under the EEC, in a generally dismissive manner, Mr James Callaghan remarked that 'There is a great deal missing from the scenario that the government has produced to us', and he was of course quite right. But that is inevitable; there is much missing, too, from the scenario presented by the opponents of the Common Market : what would the future be if Britain were to remain alone?

Mr Callaghan, Mr Foot, and certainly Mr Peter Shore would reply: 'The onus of proof that Britain will prosper does not rest upon us : it is for those who are proposing so great a change to substantiate their case, beyond a reasonable shadow of doubt; and, if that doubt remains substantial, then we shall remain as we are, and have been, perhaps making up for our isolation by our industriousness, even profiting from it to advance faster towards socialism, or alternately, towards a more dynamic capitalism, in the manner of Japan.' Mr Callaghan might, on reflection, prefer the latter course, Mr Foot and Mr Shore the former. But all it would seem, from at least recent speeches, would prefer either to adherence to the European Community.

Several arguments here intertwine, not all of them (specially not the last) particularly socialist, though all of them serious enough to be examined. 'Splendid isolation' is an attractive idea, and might appeal equally to the Left or to the Right – though there is, perhaps, little of real socialism in an argument which suggests that it is possible for any people simply to

G

cultivate their garden, and indifferently to leave their brothers in the rest of the world to sink or to swim. It is also obvious that those who opposed, and oppose, entry, risked the continuation of present trends in our society rather more than they planned for (or risked) a revolution of the Left or a 600M of the Japanese variety.

The chief response to these ideas is that the world is more of a looking-glass one than it seems at first sight: we cannot stand still, or rather even to be static implies a very high level of activity. Our competitive position has altered substantially, and for the worse, over the last generation, and will probably continue to do so, if we merely remain 'where we are' – which will thus turn out to be 'where we have never been'.

CHANGE IN UK PATTERN OF TRADE

	1958	1968	increase 1958–68
Imports	%	%	%
EEC	14	20	188
EFTA (Continental)	11	15	166
Commonwealth	35	24	40
Rest of World	40	41	108
Exports			
EEC	14	19	167
EFTA (Continental)	11	14	144
Commonwealth	38	23	14
Rest of World	37	44	125

The reasons are many: but it can easily be imagined that a country such as Britain, in the forefront of industrial or commercial innovation in the eighteenth and early nineteenth centuries, should fall behind in the twentieth, particularly when, during much of the twentieth century, international questions have preoccupied English leaders more than those of technology. Our specially long dependence upon such heavy industries as coal mining and shipbuilding naturally made it hard for us to change quickly away from these emphases, for lighter industries. Further, it is false to suppose that, either politically or economically, Britain has really 'gone it alone' in the course of the last generation. This point was made clear in the course of the Second World War: 'Britain alone' lasted from June 1940 to June 1941, it is true, but she only lasted. She did little more. Even then, she received massive economic assistance from the US; and, whether she would even have merely lasted, if Germany had not attacked Russia, or even if Japan had not subsequently attacked the US, is doubtful. The idea that it was possible to 'go-it-alone' was also rejected by Harold Wilson in 1967, as his memoirs make clear. The alternative to a new alignment is to see a continuation of the process whereby the British economy not only grows slowly, but increasingly allows the main advanced technological industries to slip away.

The alternatives to seeking a wider range for our national and economic activities should, however, be discussed, even though they seem unsatisfactory. Isolation might be possible if, like Sweden (whose GNP has grown faster since 1957 than any of the 'Six'), Britain had substantial stocks of one or two main primary products of great importance – in Sweden's case, iron ore and timber, which together enable Sweden to stand high in specialized finished goods such as knives or furniture. (Also, a population of eight million is a different proposition to ours, of fifty-seven million.) But Britain is not in that position. We have become more of a nation of shopkeepers than we ever were: our world economic position resembles that of a village shop: we sell a little of everything, and so need as many varied customers as possible, even for our minor products.

Japan's economic status is also different from that of ourselves: she is a country largely developed during the last two generations. Her home market is double that of our own, since her population is also double. She has no defence expenditure to worry about. Above all, she has been willing to sacrifice welfare for growth in a classic capitalist way. The housing in Tokyo is still primitive and pre-industrial. The universities are understaffed and crowded. The urban sprawl and pollution are uncontained. Wages are artificially low. Symbolic, perhaps, of modern Japanese attitudes to transport problems (and, perhaps, to education) is the fact that the underground hires students to pack passengers into the trains. Furthermore, Japan needs to import and to export as much as we do. Her economic situation could be radically altered, for the worse, by a great recession in the US, her main customer (as was indicated by Nixon's actions in August 1971). Japan is unlikely to keep her rate of growth as demands grow for higher living standards, better environment and a juster society.

There was, also, of course, the NAFTA alternative: the suggestion that EFTA might have been consolidated in some sort of customs union with the USA, and Canada. This possibility, with an increasingly tariff-ridden US, seems now out of the question, from a US point of view. But, even if that largely short-term objection were to vanish, there are many grave disadvantages to this variation on the theme devised by Shaw in *The Applecart*. The economic role of the US in a NAFTA would be obviously dominant. The possibilities of a creative regional policy to compensate for our own economic backwardness would be few. Cultural and political dominance would surely follow without any serious chance of Britain's being able to influence the US political system. The chances of a political union, genuinely possible within the European Community, would similarly be remote. Even if there were, a British representation as a political force in the Union would not carry much weight. The scheme would tie this country to the US just at the moment when that nation seems about to enter a trying time with internal problems of great magnitude. It is difficult to see this as a seriously appealing alternative for radical people in Great Britain.

The question of associate membership of the European Community has been raised. Professor Kaldor has suggested this idea as an alternative, until 'the present agricultural mess is cleared up (which may take ten to twenty years)'. This, he adds with apocalyptic gloom, is essential to avoid payment of 'tribute' to the CAP which would impose a burden upon us as great as that imposed on Germany by the Treaty of Versailles. The disadvantages to this course are, however, great. The same

political objections apply as with NAFTA. Political developments would occur in Europe by which we should be bound,
but over which we should have no control.

It could, doubtless, be maintained that a consequence of
total isolation would be to increase our economic problems to
such an extent as to cause serious social or political instability.
But no one in their senses could seriously advocate this
possibility. Even if such a person could entertain a cynical pre-
sumption that there would be, afterwards, a great opportunity
for state socialism, there would be no certainty that that would
be the result, nor that it would be a uniquely British form of it,
insulated from the rest of the world. Anyone who has gambled
that disruption offers an opportunity to the Left have often
found that the Right sees the opportunity more quickly: as
occurred in Italy, Germany and Spain, between the wars, as
countless socialists have found in South America, and as the
New Left found in France in 1968. Even if, against the odds,
the Left did profit in this manner, there would, in the circumstances, be many long-term difficulties; and if the subsequent
government responsible were to remain democratic, it would
surely turn towards the US for help, as Mr Wilson's government often did, but perhaps being obliged to enter upon a more
permanent and subservient relation with the US than socialists
would normally consider desirable. This was what Mr Eric
Heffer feared when he remarked in May 1967: 'The alternative
would, in my view, mean our ultimately becoming a satellite of
the US'; or, if the government were able – and perhaps, after
all, that alternative cannot logically be excluded – to dispense
with democracy, it would no doubt turn towards the Soviet
Union.

Such a Britain would, after all, have to rely on commerce as
much as she does today; her competitiveness against, for
example, Japan might slump – for Britain as yet has not had
to feel the full force of Japanese competition, and, in the long
run, who knows, a contrite government might, a generation or
so hence, be prevailed upon, in even weaker conditions than
these of now, to seek association with, or even membership of,

the European Community, as would seem most natural for geographical reasons alone. A socialist Britain would doubtless be a fine thing; but it would be an illusion to suppose that it could solve all our problems; indeed, a democratic socialist Britain would, probably, not survive long on the edge of a continent which was abrasively anti-socialist, nor of a world economy dominated by multinational companies. 'Go-it-alone?' said Mr James Callaghan in May 1967, 'It would be possible, but we should need to follow autarchic and self-sufficient policies, which would fragment our relations with Europe and maybe with others.' Most people would put it stronger. Indeed, Mr Callaghan did himself when in 1971 he staked his claim as the leader of the anti-European Left. The alternative to the EEC, he said in July 1971, before the Labour party's special conference, was to 'run the economy flat out for five years'. As Tom Nairn wisely pointed out, this was as if one of the generals of Dunkirk had crawled onto Dover Beach and announced his strategy for winning the war: send a new BEF to France.[42]

All these alternatives are really mythical ones, as acts of policy. The chances of a serious alternative to the EEC are really non-existent. Our economic isolation, or at least our independence, has after all been limited during the generation since 1945, and in reality since 1914: Stanley Henig put this point in the Labour Party's Common Market Conference in July 1971: 'I think there is not the slightest doubt, and ought not to be in anybody's mind, that the basic reason why so many things went wrong [during the last Labour government] was the economic vulnerability of this country to matters outside our control. We... remember the number of times that government spokesmen came to us and said: "There is nothing we can do about this situation economically, it is out of our control".' Of course, people have short memories: but can there be any doubt that the economy was several times 'blown off course' during the years of apparent opportunity between 1964 and 1970 by factors beyond our own control? The moral, which was long ago learned by countries who have been small and powerless before great foreign economic strength, may understandably not yet be fully evident to Englishmen, particularly those with recollections which stretch back beyond the Second World War and who, consequently, cannot quite believe that this new impotence would have been a permanent characteristic of our future if we had remained outside the Community.

In the recent past, we have had, in many ways, the worst of all worlds: our own economic base has been too small for our prosperity, and so it has not given us independence. We have been pushed hither and thither by the fluctuations of world trading conditions, over which we have had less and less power, and, in the last ten years, we have oscillated between the US economic system and the European one – a situation which has been extraordinarily uncomfortable and likely to be ours indefinitely, for all the rhetoric of Mr Shore, Mr Powell and Mr Foot, unless we take definite action now. Winston Churchill hoped, as the country hoped, probably, after 1945, that the three concentric circles of Europe, America and the Commonwealth would revolve around us: but the politics of this metaphor has been as unsatisfactory as its geometry. We have, in fact, fallen between three stools, not dominated three circles; and we have been fortunate to have a chance of thinking about it once or twice before it was too late. Once again the history of the German Zollverein comes to mind; it was only narrowly that Britain, in the 1960s, succeeded in avoiding the fate of Austria-Hungary, a great power of the past similarly preoccupied by her internal affairs in the 1860s. Austria refused to join at the beginning of the Zollverein, and then applied too late. The consequence was her defeat in war in the 1860s, the collapse of her society in the 1920s, the establishment in the 1940s upon what had been once her territory of Auschwitz, Sachsenhausen and other centres of infamy, and the loss of much of her territory to domination by Russia, or to Russia directly.

Conclusion

The purpose of this study was to persuade those forward-looking people who are opposed to British accession to the European Economic Community that they are wrong; that the lives of the British people will, on the whole, be happier, more interesting, and more secure, once we have joined than before; and that the real aims of the Labour party, the main radical political movement in the country, will be more easily achieved by acting within Europe than by remaining without. The book has also argued that Britain has almost as much to offer Europe as Europe has to offer to her. It is directed both at those who, over the last months, have resisted the idea of joining Europe, at all costs; and towards those who have been willing to join Europe 'if the terms are right' – though the latter clearly include some who, with varying degrees of sincerity, argue about the terms in order to conceal their distrust or dislike of the idea.

I believe too that, in the discussion about the opportunities for radical democracy or for democratic socialism in a united Europe, some general ideas will have appeared, among them some which go beyond the limited matter of contemporary debate, thereby confirming the comment of the Labour Party's National Executive, at the time of Harold Macmillan's first application, on Britain's behalf, to join the European Economic Community, that that was 'a great and imaginative conception' of unprecedented importance for us all. For this reason, the book is addressed to those who have already accepted the idea that Britain should join the European Community, as well as those who have not. Among the former, there are many who, it seems, have accepted the idea as the best political or economic solution to the problem of Britain's future, but have done so without enthusiasm, even without knowledge. A glazed look sometimes steals, at the mention of the Community, even over the faces of those who have supported it and its implications for ten years. It is not that too little has been said, but too much. It is not that the bureaucrats of Europe have been too secretive, but that their absence of secrets has rendered them publicly duller than they need have been. The politics of Europe have scarcely been made to live warmly in the imaginations even of Europe's friends. 'One cannot imagine anyone setting out consciously to go to Brussels,' one of Ronald Firbank's characters said, with customary affectation, in the 1920s, and that point of view has influenced many who would vote in a referendum, if there were to be one, to join the Community. They, too, will, I hope, find that their point of view was comprehended here.

It is difficult to accept that the Labour party cannot change its mind again over the question of the Community. Essentially, they have already done so once. The German social democrats had doubts about the European Coal and Steel Community in 1952 but, becoming active members of the Community's Assembly, voted for the Common Market and Euratom in 1957. The Italian socialists (and even the Italian communists) had a similar change of heart. Even the Spanish socialists recently called for Spain to join the Community. Thus the British Labour movement seems to be acting fully in the tradition of European socialism by being suspicious to begin with of European integration – providing, however, that there is one day a change of heart. After all, even if there were anything so unfortunate as a promise by the Labour party to withdraw from the EEC if it gets back to power, the odds are long that that promise would ever be carried out. If General de Gaulle did not withdraw France from the EEC, when he came to power and disliked it so much, in the late fifties, and when the EEC was so new, it is inconceivable that Britain should withdraw in the 1970s, once she has entered. It is likely that, by the time that a new Labour government comes to power, neither Britain, nor any other European country, will be able to withdraw from the Community without damaging herself too severely to make the idea a realistic one.

This study does not dwell much on past wrangles. But it is impossible, nevertheless, to avoid being struck by the singularly narrow nature of many of the arguments deployed by anti-Marketeers on the Left in British politics. In 1962, the National Executive of the Labour Party was speaking of our weak balance of payments, our great debts, and so on, as being reasons to shy away from the gate of Europe. But these factors, though considerable, and, indeed, though considerable for many years, are mean, when placed against the dramatic idea of joining a large and expanding customs union which, even in 1961 evidently had long-term political significance: and which now is opening up considerable political opportunities. A week may be a long time in politics, in Mr Harold Wilson's phrase. But, in political history, ten years is a short time, and the voters are entitled, surely, to some predictions by statesmen as to what they think should be happening by the end of this century, now not much more than twenty-five years ahead: just as the voters are entitled to tell them what they think, if they can only find a channel of communication.

Short-sighted arguments are particularly mistaken, since Labour can hardly claim to have faithfully represented public opinion in this matter. The British public, if the polls are right, has been understandably inconsistent over the whole question of the EEC. Why, for instance, did public opinion move from being seven to ten in favour of the EEC in 1967, to about three to five against in 1971? Partly, surely, because the electorate believed that Britain would not be able to join even if she wanted to. Once the idea of accession began to assume reality, the vote in favour increased. Further, the polls are clearly open to much argument: even when seven to ten were in favour, only one out of ten could name all the countries who were members of the Community.

It is also difficult to forget that many of the arguments in this study can be supported by the quotation of some remark or speech by one or other of Labour's leaders during the late government, and particularly by Mr Harold Wilson and Mr James Callaghan. Thus it is obvious that these men have not got to think things out anew in order to appreciate the right policy but have simply to go back to their earlier, if not always their first, thoughts.

One difficulty may have been that the question as to whether or not to join the European Community has seemed an issue in foreign policy, and it has been dealt with by the Foreign Office. Labour has, therefore, approached it, as it usually does questions of foreign policy, from either a traditionalist or a fundamentalist attitude – the former signifying the national interest, the latter signifying the interests of internationalism in general, the international working-class anti-capitalism and anti-militarism. In these respects, the anti-Marketeers have seemed traditionalist, though often on the Left. But the European Community, just as it is neither a matter of Left nor Right, is neither explicitly a matter of domestic or foreign policy: it spans both. In a sense, too, it also transcends politics, since the consequences are such as to impose considerable, though not overwhelming, problems to the national parties which have grown to dominate the parliaments of nation states. (The same point may be made about two other new twentieth-century considerations: colour, and the environment, both of which were discussed earlier.)

There have admittedly always been a group of Labour and radical people who, ever since the idea of European integration was first mooted after the Second World War, have been consistent on this issue; equally, there has always been a group, a majority, perhaps, among the Labour party, who have been cautious and non-committal, not knowing what to do for the best, for their country, their party, as for themselves; and, in 1963, on the death of Hugh Gaitskell, the Parliamentary Labour Party elected one of these undecided men as their leader. From that decision, much else flowed. Had that election occurred at another time, rather than just after General de Gaulle's veto of Mr Macmillan's application to join the

Community, perhaps the contest for the Labour leadership would have been decided differently: but, in January 1963, the European issue seemed a dead one, and a leader who had taken no real view on the subject seemed the best.

Leaving all these things aside, however, it is essential now to appreciate that Europe offers a really exciting and radical opportunity to re-form our social, economic and political circumstances. The present time is one of those infrequent occasions in the history of human communities when new institutions can be shaped; and it is at this moment, that most of Europe's new institutions and habits will be forged.

The early years of new undertakings are the critical ones, since it is usually more difficult to change practices which have become settled than it is to start from the beginning. It is, of course, sad to think that a Labour government might have been, but was not, responsible for the inspiration of, and invigoration of, this new stage; but the Labour movement could still play a creative role in Opposition, as the European socialist parties have consistently done, acting in the firm belief that, in present circumstances, a democratic socialist, or radical, Europe can be created; whereas, even radicalism in one country is probably now an impractical, as well as an insufficiently ambitious, aim. But there is a more fundamental point too, which underlies much of the argument that has occurred : that is, that it has been found impossible to change radically for the better the existing unrepresentative, and excessively acquisitive, structure of society within the bounds of the present nation state, as it has developed during the last two generations. This fact may not be easily appreciated by those active in day-to-day politics. But it is obvious to the electorate, and to Labour voters particularly. No one surely can believe that another Labour government of the same temperament that existed from 1964 to 1970 would be any more successful than the last one was in resolving Britain's economic and social problems outside the Community.

In one way, it is rather desirable that Britain should be led into Europe by Edward Heath and the Conservative party.

The Conservatives are by tradition the nationalist party in Britain. Had it been they who had been in opposition to a Labour bid to join Europe, as would have occurred if Labour had won the election of 1970, the hostility might have been much uglier and more heartfelt than it has been: Mr Heath might have been dropped, Mr Enoch Powell perhaps raised, if not to power, at least upwards, and the noises of Right-wing nationalism would have growled more insistently and more effectively if it had been a Labour prime minister who was dismantling our national sovereignty. As it is, we have seen instead the flourishing of a plant which seems exotic, though it is a good deal more common than is sometimes supposed: Left-wing nationalism.

Two main arguments are customarily put forward for joining the EEC: the one is political, the second economic. There is also a third argument, which might be described as social.

The political argument is that the European Economic Community and its related undertakings (Euratom, the Coal and Steel Community, and so on) foreshadows a new multinational political union whose character Britain could hope to influence, presumably for the better, if she were within it, and by which she would be affected, probably for the worse, if she were outside.

The economic argument suggests that Britain, a nation more dependent upon trade than any other of comparable size save Japan, and with, therefore, an economy where prosperity at home is more closely related to exports than most, now needs a larger home market in which to sell her goods: and that the European Economic Community offers the only sensible solution.

The social argument suggests that in respect of access to social services, changing attitudes to colour and to female workers, trade union relationships, the ordinary citizen has more to gain from the European Community than he (or she) has to lose.

The first two arguments have negative characteristics as well as positive ones: some believe that the European political union is not a very desirable enterprise (being likely to be dominated

by Germany or France), but that it is better to make an adjust-
ment, while we can, to a potentially strong, even if disagreeable,
political grouping. Similarly, some approach the economic
reasoning in the belief that 'unless we do something we shall be
sunk', and that the opening to Europe is the most appealing
one – though only the best of a bad series of choices.

Ever since the idea of joining the EEC was broached, in the
late 1950s, people have distinguished their attitudes to it by
economic or political reasons: it has been common to hear
people, including politicians, saying that they supported or
opposed the idea on political or on economic grounds. They
still speak this way, and it is a convenient approach to the
matter, though few would have full confidence in any politician
who separated the two subjects altogether.

In dealing with economics, we are dealing with predictions,
expectations and plans: even with desires. It is, therefore,
comprehensible that different economists should reach different
conclusions; and interesting, but no more than that, that a poll
of British academic economists in October 1971, showed an
almost fifty-fifty division over whether entry into the EEC
would, or would not, be beneficial to the economy; although
business economists and foreign – that is, US and continental
European – economists are generally favourable, usually enthusiastically so. Furthermore, the range of economic decisions
affecting the Common Market are so many, and have so many
ramifications, that a political organization of potentially great
power has been born, with long-term consequences, which are
probably already irreversible. Some political consequences, including the idea of direct elections to the European Assembly,
were indeed implicit in the text of the Treaty of Rome. Political
union is likely within a generation, perhaps sooner. 'Supra-
nationality . . . is inscribed in the future . . . and in my view can
only develop.' Thus François Mitterand, still the only effective
leader of the French socialists to be found. The Paris summit
called for European union by 1980 has to be faced.

Here, there was a substantial difference between Britain and
the other countries who joined the EEC in the 1950s; we join,

it would seem, from the justificatory speeches of all our leaders, primarily for economic reasons, and accept the political consequences as an afterthought; on the Continent, they saw political union as a goal at the beginning.

It is admittedly possible that Harold Wilson took the lessons of the crisis in the Community during 1965–6 into account when he made his own first application to join in 1967 (despite Lord Wigg's comment in his memoirs, that he thought only of a short-term political gain). The Luxembourg Agreement of 1966, after all, led to a tacit agreement to disagree between the 'Five' and France: the latter insisted on her freedom to use a veto, and to avoid majority votes, on 'issues of vital national interest'. Nevertheless, after 1 January 1973, Britain will be subject to a series of rules and directions with which the British parliament had nothing to do in their formation: that is the consequence of our cold shoulder to the Community during its formation in the 1950s. It is obvious that the British parliament will, afterwards, have a voice in the discussion of the same rules, will be able to modify them, improve them, and even substitute better ones for them. 'By far the greater part of British domestic law,' as Harold Wilson put it in 1967, 'will remain untouched after our entry,' as will many of our legal practices. It is our good fortune indeed that much of the political side of the European Community remains to be constructed; something we owe to de Gaulle, who was the main, though not the only voice against further political integration in the 1960s as well as stopping our own entry in 1963 and 1967. But in a few years, such national action within the Community will almost certainly be impossible.

The conclusion to this discussion can be simply summarized: the European Community offers a new method of harnessing large-scale public power. Providing that the progressive parties of Europe seize the opportunity, they have an excellent chance of securing that that power is creatively and generously used. The British Labour party, and other progressive movements, have everything to gain from closer associations with parties whose intellectual curiosity and traditions have been often more demanding, if sometimes less fortunate, than our own. Very many things need to be done in our societies, as in those of our neighbours, that probably will not be achieved unless we are able to operate on a larger scale. We should attempt to do so, and, at the same time, ensure that the amplitude of the vision does not bring clumsy or tyrannous treatment of ordinary people.

There are two further general points to be made. The European Community seems to some to threaten to become a kind of supranational juggernaut, in which all the faults of central governments, or of large institutions in general, are likely to be seen writ large. This should be a serious preoccupation for Marketeers, and it is one which has here been discussed at length, particularly when talking of the international company and regional questions. The only simple answer to the question of alienation from the political life is an old one: politics. Democratic politics are, after all, at worst a fascinating game: one of the many disadvantages of authoritarian regimes is that they deny precisely that element of play within the system.

It is not entirely superfluous to linger on the democratic implications of social democracy, or democratic socialism – two ideas which I take to be synonymous. Many of those who vote Labour in British elections are democrats before they are socialists. They accept, that is, the ideas that if their views are insufficiently persuasive they will not be able to put them into practice. This idea has a number of shortcomings, it is true, such as that very often it is difficult to put over complicated opinions in a popular manner. The process has, moreover, among other advantages, the idea that governments can be changed without violence, and the possibility that a man's political career may be ruined if he makes too many mistakes.

Most democratic socialist voters would prefer to live under a democratic conservative rule than an authoritarian socialist one. Of course, a great deal more can be said about this subject, but one historical comment might be added: democracy, as we now define it, as universal suffrage, dates only from the twentieth century and, therefore, is far from the old-fashioned system that

Fascists and modern 'revolutionaries' alike make it out to be. Democracy is still in an experimental stage, whereas absolutism, which, in one form or another, is still represented sometimes as a novel, and efficient, alternative, is a conventional and outworn method. That point becomes particularly clear when it is remembered that democracy has developed in this century during a terrible series of tumults: the two world wars, vast migrations, enormous changes in industrial methods, technology, and in the physical shape of the countryside, not to speak of, even in advanced countries, relapses into authoritarian rule.

This argument is, as it happens, almost a paraphrase of a lecture on 'democratic values' by Aneurin Bevan in 1950, but there is little to add to it. It expresses the general attitude towards democracy of one of its most able practitioners, and it should be borne in mind, when meeting the complaints, or even the violence, of those on both the extreme Left and the extreme Right.

The whole idea of the European Community will doubtless continue to be opposed by different groups in the Labour party, who will wish to draw out, and continue to hold that line, even if it plainly ceases to be a popular one: and there will be those who will wish to withdraw, unless there are new negotiations. Such discontented groups might make common ground internationally, and it is only too easy to imagine some future congress at which Clive Jenkins and Enoch Powell address the IRA on the subject of European integration. Yet, if such were to occur, it would go a long way to prove the integrationists' point: namely, that it is through unity that real diversity can be secured. These new Jacobites will linger on, no doubt for many years, in the same self-destructive frame of mind that characterized Bonnie Prince Charlie and his followers for a generation following the forty-five: and, perhaps, when they are dead and forgotten, a new Sir Walter will arise to dignify their groping with the false name of romance.

A simple summary has been made of the economical reasons for European action by Professor Sasse: 'Economic problems no longer remain national. The world monetary situation calls for action on a wider [and] regional basis. Big industry, especially the so-called multinational enterprises, are able to dodge national measures without difficulty. The ambition to develop technology on a national level can only lead to increasing backwardness. The destruction of the biosphere is not checked by national frontiers. . . . The relations with the Third World call for common action. And, finally, also a lasting social system calls for an order of magnitude which is less susceptible to disruption than the small societies of the present European states.'[43]

Looking ahead in a general sense, it is surely essential to revive some sense of broad optimism in our political affairs. This is a state of mind, almost as much as anything else. Vast attention is paid to the evil side of modern society, rightly in some circumstances, but so often that those who continue to believe in the possibility of rational conduct in politics are often defensive or apologetic. The two world wars, with their Nazi and Stalinist accompaniments, were admittedly terrible setbacks to a belief in progress. The continued and increased poverty in the Third World remains a reproach to our generation. Still, the last twenty-five years have seen an enormous leap forward in the style of living of much of the human race. Major wars have been averted, and may even be a thing of the past. In a few more years, the cynicism, querulousness and self-distrust of the late twentieth century could well disappear. It is difficult not to read of life in Europe before 1914 without a certain envy of the stability and the self-confidence of the majority of the upper class of those days. The scientific revolution, given humane, generous and open-minded political decisions, could within a short time bring such stability and such self-confidence to the lives of most people. It will doubtless not do so in the name of any particular revolutionary or conservative dogma. But it could well do so all the same without, however, the aggressive nationalism and the upper-class arrogance that characterized the attitudes of those of our grandfathers fortunate enough to live within the charmed circles. Comfort, optimisim and self-confidence do not derive from exclusiveness, or, otherwise, the artistocracy would have had a better time in the tenth century than they did in the nineteenth. Nor is religion the key to social harmony, as, once again, the decline in faith in the nineteenth century proved conclusively. Wide benefits and advantages, and lives of prosperity and leisure, accompanied by the possibility of extraordinary scientific adventure, lie ahead, if we seize our opportunities in scarcely more than the right spirit. In the formation of this right spirit and in ensuring that it is contagious, the enlarged European Community will surely play a great part.

Notes

1 Norman Hart and Ernest Wistrich, *Europe out of the Impasse,* (Fabian pamphlet 1969), p. 4.
2 Proudhon, *Du Principe Fédératif,* (Paris 1863), p. 52.
3 Spinelli, *Government and Opposition,* (April-July 1967).
4 Walter Hallstein in *Problems of British Entry into the EEC,* (Chatham House, London 1969), p. 96.
5 Willy Brandt, *In exile,* (London 1971), p. 26.
6 Spinelli, *op. cit.*
7 Roy Jenkins, *Afternoon on the Potomac,* (London 1972), p. 35.
8 *Britain and the EEC,* supplementary report of the TUC General Council to the 102nd Annual TUC, (1970).
9 Paul Johnson, *New Statesman,* (7 May 1972).
10 Hugh Seton Watson, *The Russian Empire, 1801-1917,* (OUP, London 1966), p. 620.
11 Roy Jenkins, *op. cit.,* p. 33.
12 See Michael Stewart, *New Europe,* (May 1972).
13 Michael Niblock in *EEC: National Parliaments in Community Decision-making,* (Chatham House, London 1971), p. 81.
14 Gerda Zellentin, *Government and Opposition,* (April-July 1967).
15 Professor Christopher Sasse, *Institutional Structure of Europe,* Introductory Report to European Movement Conference, (May 1972).
16 *The Times* (2 May 1972).
17 Lord Gladwyn, *New Europe,* (May 1972).
18 Ivor Richard, Alan Williams, Geoffrey Williams, Glyn Mathias, *Europe or the Open Sea,* (London 1971).
19 Y. Harkabi, *Survival,* (October 1969).
20 François Duchêne, 'Europe's Role in World Peace' in Richard Mayne, *Europe Tomorrow,* (London 1972), p. 38.
21 Ivor Richard, Alan Williams, Geoffrey Williams, Glyn Mathias, *op. cit.,* p. 122.
22 John Hatch, *Venture,* (November 1971).

23 Labour and the Common Market Statement by the NEC, (29 September 1962).
24 Ian Little, 'International Tax on the Rich to help the Poor', *Times*, (9 May 1972).
25 *Venture*, (November 1971).
26 Coventry and District Engineering employers association: *Labour Relations and employment conditions in the EEC*, (1972).
27 Ernest Mandel, *Europe versus America*, (London 1970), p. 122.
28 John Wallace, *Times*, (2 May 1972).
29 In Pinder, *The Economics of Europe*, (London 1971), p. 48-49.
30 Ivor Richard, Alan Williams, Geoffrey Willaims, Glyn Mathias, *op. cit.*, p. 10.
32 Foreign Direct Investment in EFTA Countries, EFTA Secretariat, (Geneva 1969).
33 Stanislas M. Yassukovich, *Capital Flows* in Pinder, *op. cit.*
34 See Heidrick and Stuggles, *Britain and the Common Market*, a Survey of American Company reactions, (London 1971), and also J. H. Dunning, *The Location of International Firms in an enlarged EEC*, Reading Discussion papers in Economics, no. 35.
35 In Pinder, *op. cit.*, p. 44-45.
36 Christopher Layton, *Technology and Industry*, in Mayne *op. cit.*
37 Mayne, *op. cit.*, p. 103.
38 Text in *Guardian*, (11 April 1972).
39 Phlipponeau, in Mayne, *op. cit.*, p. 152.
40 *Country Life*, (27 April 1972).
41 Miguel Garcia, *Franco's Prisoner*, (London 1972), p. 110.
42 *New Left Review*, (October 1971).
43 Sasse, *op. cit.*, p. 6.

Index

Abse, Leo, 38
Adenauer, Dr, 8
Aerospace industry, 127, 135
Africa,, 79, 82, 85
Agriculture, 113, 143, 165–175
  British, 107
  decrease in jobs, 97
  employment in, 165
  European, 17
Agricultural Fund of the Community, 173
Aid, 77–83
Aircraft, 71, 114
  noise, 159, 160
  safety, 154
Algerian workers in France, 91
Almirante, Giorgio, 64
American Continental Can Company, 150
'Americanization', 133
Anglo-Italian declaration on direct elections, 33
Apulia, 173
Aquitaine, 144, 173
Arab World, 78
Argentine, 169
Arisha Agreement, 1968–1969, 78
Atomic energy, 133
Australia, 127
Austria, 51, 54, 58, 151, 187

Balogh, Lord, 119
Banco di Roma, 150
Banks, banking, 108, 150
  nationalization of, 118, 119
Barley, 169

Barre, Raymond, 162
Basle Agreement, the, 124
Basque country, 145, 146
Bavaria, 145, 153, 173
Beamish, Sir Tufton, 33
Beef, 169
Belgium, 14, 18, 36, 45, 80, 94, 142
Bellini, James, 117, 131
Benn, Anthony Wedgwood, 23
Berlinguer, Enrico, 42
Bevan, Aneurin, 155, 197
'Beveridge' system, 98
Borschette, Albert, 101
Bottini, Reg, 156
Bottomley, Arthur, 133
Bowden, Herbert, 60
Brandt, Willy, 13, 14, 18, 58, 63, 67, 106
Brazil, 82
Breton farmers, 16
Bretton Woods, 140
Brezhnev, L., 67
Briand, Aristide, 8
Brighton Trades Union Congress, 14
British Petroleum, 118
Brown, Godfrey, 174
Bruck, Camille, 138
Brussels, 19, 25, 44, 45, 145, 189
Brussels Treaty, 74
Budget, Community, 134, 166
Bureaucracy, expansion of, 119, 120
Burma, 82

Callaghan, James, 181, 186, 191
Canada, 72, 184

CAP (Common Agricultural Policy), 48, 127, 143, 167, 170, 171, 184
Capital of Europe, 44–45
Capital, capitalism, 108, 127, 129
English, 117
foreign, 134
free flow of, 155
Car, the private, 152–3, 158, 161, 163
Car industry, British, 113, 114, 127
Car workers of Europe, 102
Caribbean sugar problem, 79, 81
Carrington, Lord, 66
Castle, Mrs Barbara, 110, 154
Catalonia, 145, 146
Centralization, excessive, 154
Centre Européen de Recherches Nucléaires (CERN), 151
'Centre-periphery' hypothesis, 146, 147, 148
Chad, 82
Chambers, see Parliament, European
Channel Islands, the, 156
Chemical industry, 114
Chile, 119
China, 53, 70, 85
Christian Democrat Party, European, 43
Churchill, Sir Winston, 8, 68, 187
CIA, the, 76
CII, 130
City of London, the, 107, 108, 109
Clapham, Michael, 167
Clark, Colin, 147
Clothing firms, British, 106
Coal industry, 97, 119, 143, 154
Coal & Steel Community, European, 5, 10, 189, 193
Common Assembly of the, 28
Fund, 143–144
Coal & Steel companies, 104
Co-determination, see Mitbestimmung
Collaboration in mixed economy, 142
Colour, problem of, 193
Combat, 8

Combat and direct forces, 71
Commerce, 12, 112, 171
Commerzbank, 150
Commission, the European, 16, 18, 19, 20–25, 27, 28, 32, 34, 44, 46, 47, 80, 100, 101, 105, 110, 111, 112, 113, 115, 131, 132, 135, 142, 149, 150, 159, 161, 162, 166, 171, 179
Commissioners, 10, 14, 15, 16, 21, 24, 25
Commonwealth, the, 77, 78, 114, 116, 121, 127, 174, 182, 187
'Associables', 79
Companies, British, 107, 108, 109
French, 108
US, 134
Company, European, 131
Statute, 105, 131
Competition, 125
rules of, under Treaty of Rome, 119
Computers, 114, 127, 134
Japanese, 136
Concorde, the, 72, 135
Confederation, 5, 17, 25
Confederation of British Industries, 93, 167
Confederation of Shipbuilding and Engineering Unions, 93
Conscription, 75
Conway, James, 103
Cost of living, 171, 172, 173, 174
see also food, price of
Cotton manufacturing firms, British, 106
Council of Europe, 29
assembly of, 34, 36
Council of Ministers, 16, 17, 18, 20, 21, 24, 25, 27, 28, 31, 32, 34, 167
Court of Justice, European, 16, 20, 21, 27, 31, 44, 45, 115
Courtaulds, 129
Coventry engineering industry, 95
Crédit Lyonnais, 150
Crosland, Anthony, 8, 120
Cuba, 13, 62, 74, 82

Currency, European, 11, 128, 138, 140
Czechoslovakia, 60, 71, 177

Davignon Report, 47
Defence, 30, 61, 66–76, 183
Defence White Papers, 1966 and 1972, 67
Dehousse, Fernand, 31
Democracy, social, 46, 117, 196
Democratization of Community, 18–19
Denmark, 36, 169
Devaluation, 138
Diet, 158, 173
Diplomas, mutual recognition of, 32
Disarmament, 84
Douglas Home, Sir Alec, 10, 11, 12, 19, 80
Duchêne, François, 70, 83
Dunlop, 130
Dunlop-Pirelli Company, 102, 150

Earnings see Wages
East Germany, 52, 60
Eastern Europe, 52, 60, 61, 62, 67, 163, 180
Economic Affairs, Department of, 178
Economic and Social Committee, 15–16
Economic planning, 176–180
Economist, The, 44
education, 88–91, 158
EFTA see European Free Trade Area
Eifel region, 144, 145
Eire see Ireland
Electrical industries, 114, 119, 127, 130
energy, policy for, 154
Engineering Union, British, 103
ENI, 141
Environment, the, 9, 23, 159–64, 166
Euratom, 5, 189, 193
research budget of, 161
Eurodollar, the, 53, 107, 132

Eurogroup, 69
'Europa' see currency, European
European Communities Bill, 1, 2
European Development Fund, 78, 81, 82
European Economic and Social Committee, 16, 25, 26
European Free Trade Area (EFTA), 6, 51, 54, 104, 106, 113, 121, 169, 182, 184
European Investment Bank, 57
European Security Conference, 58, 59, 75, 180
Treaty, 67
Europemballage, 131, 150
Evans, Moss, 102
Evans, Roger, 46
exchange rates, 138

Family allowances, 98
farmers, pensions and retraining facilities, 167
farms (see also agriculture), economically viable, 167
English, 165
in EEC, status of, 166
buildings, 166
modernization of, 167
farming methods, 71
mixed, 169
policy, common, 32
Feather, Vic, 93, 157
Federal Republic of Germany, 14, 63–4, 65, 69, 74, 78, 80, 85, 86, 94, 103, 110, 114, 142, 143, 145, 146, 154, 163, 164, 166, 177, 179, 183, 185, 189, 194
coal industry, 119
food, 174
trade with Commonwealth, 78
Federal Reserve System, 140
Federal Trust study group, 137, 138
Federalism/federation, 5, 7, 8, 9, 10, 11, 17, 25, 26, 29, 41, 60, 70, 83
Fiat, 106
Financial Times, The, 109
Finland, 51, 54, 73, 157
fiscal policies, common, 156

fishing, deep sea, 171
  twelve-mile limit, 171
Flemish interests, 142
Food, 168, 172, 173, 174, 175
  prices, 167, 168, 171, 172
  surpluses, 166
  tax, 156, 157
Foot, Michael, 1, 40, 181, 187
Ford, Henry, 129
  129
Ford Motor Company, 126, 127,
Foreign investment, 134
Foreign workers, migrant workers,
  9, 32, 37, 89, 100, 101
France, 12, 14, 25, 36, 45, 69, 78,
  80, 81, 85, 86, 94, 103, 110, 141,
  142, 143, 156, 165, 166, 169,
  178, 179, 185, 194, 195
  Anglo-French relations, 69
  coal mines, 119
  economy, 113
  electricity, 119
  fod, 174
Franco, General Francisco, 56
free movement of labour see labour
Free movement of persons, 12
French Sahara, 78
'fringe benefits', 94, 102

Gabon, 78
Gaitskell, Hugh, 1, 84, 191
Galbraith, J. K., 177
GATT (General Agreement on
  Tariffs and Trade), 48, 179
Gaulle, General de, 5, 7, 10, 11, 49,
  67, 69, 189, 191, 195
Gaullism, 53
Gehlen, General, 76
General Motors, 130
George-Brown, Lord, 178
Germany, West, see Federal Repub-
  lic of Germany
Ghana, 78
glass industries, 114
Grantham, Ray, 78
Greece, 23, 51, 56, 69
  association, 57
Gromyko, A., 67

'Growth pole', 142
Grundig–Consten case, 115
Guardian, The, 10m, 108fn

Habsburg empire, 86
Hailsham, Lord, 12
Haiti, 82
Hallstein, Walter, 10
Hammarskjöld, Dag, 23
Harkabi, General, 62
Harmel, Pierre, 80
Hart, Norman, 60
Hatch, John, 77
Healey, Denis, 68
health, 9
Health Service, British, 89, 99
Heath, Edward, 6, 10, 11, 53, 59,
  66, 69, 72, 192, 193
Heffer, Eric, 185
Henig, Stanley, 186
Herbert, Sir Alan, 38
Hirsch, Étienne, 22
Hoesch Steel Company, 130
holidays, 102, 154
Holland see Netherlands
Hoogovens Steel Company, 130
housing, 89, 160, 164
  prices, 162
  tax, 157
Housing Finance Act, 162
Hudson Institute, the, 117
Hungary, 61, 71, 177, 180

IBM (International Business Machines), 130
Iceland, 54, 69
ICI (Imperial Chemical Industries),
  149
ILO (International Labour Office),
  175
IMF (International Monetary
  Fund), 82
immigrant workers, 91, 100
immigrants, Commonwealth, 91
import control, 168
income tax, 156
incomes, industrial, 166
India, 78

Indian Ocean, 79
Industrial Development Corporation, 141, 179fn
Industrial Reorganization Corporation, 134
Industrie Riunite Electrodomestici (IRE), 150
inflation, 178
information, dissemination of by European government, 43–44
INI (Institut National d'Industrie), 141
Institut de Dévelopment Industriel, 108
insurance business, London, 109
insurance schemes, 118
intelligence services, 75–6
International Brigades, in Spain, 9
international organizations, European policies in, 47
International Sugar Agreement, 80
investment, 155
investment trusts, 108
IRA (Irish Republican Army), 64, 197
Ireland, 36, 39, 62, 143, 154, 169
isolation, splendid (go-it-alone), 181, 183, 185, 186
Israel, 13, 53
Italy, 14, 17, 33, 36, 69, 78, 80, 85, 86, 94, 102, 110, 114, 141, 142, 145, 150, 154, 156, 165, 177, 185, 189
    food, 174
    nationalization, 119
    refrigerators, 106, 113
    washing machines, 106
Ivory Coast, 80

Japan, 48, 49, 52, 53, 70, 102, 157, 164, 183, 184, 185, 193
    car industry, 114
    computers, 136
Jay, Douglas, 155
Jeuda, Diana, 172
Jenkins, Clive, 14, 64, 197
Jenkins, Roy, 13–14, 29, 49, 79, 124
Johnson, Paul, 14, 64

Joll, James, 90
Jones, Jack, 46
Journalists, journalism, 43–4

Kahn, Hermann, 117
Kaldor, Professor N., 48, 107, 145, 184
Kennedy, President, 43
Kenya, 78
Kirchheimer, O., 37

Labour, 155
    conditions, 101
    mobility of, 9, 100, 101, 143
Labour Party, 37, 46
    Government White Paper on EEC, 135
    election manifestoes, 2
    Common Market Conference, 78, 133, 149, 186
    Conference, 156
land, 162
    public ownership of, 163
language, French as second, 90–1
Layton, Christopher, 6, 113, 136, 151
legal profession, the British, 87
Liberal Party (see Parties, European), European, 43
Libya, 82
licensing system, Community, 110
Liechtenstein, 156
light industries, 97
Lille, 142fn
Little, Ian, 83
Liverpool, 102
London, 145
    as commercial centre, 109
    as commercial centre for European Parliament, 45
López Rodó, Laureano, 55
Lorraine, 143, 145, 147
lorries, 110, 111, 152
'Lotharingia', 146
Luxembourg, 25, 36, 44, 45, 109
Luxembourg Agreement, The, 195
luxuries, 158

McGovern, Senator, 48, 57
Mack Smith, Denis, 144
Mackintosh, John, 96
Macleod, Ian, 157
Macmahon Act, 72
Macmillan, Harold, 1, 6, 11, 188, 191
Madagascar, 79
Madrid, 145
Mandel, Ernest, 105, 134, 150
Mann, Golo, 163
Mansholt, Dr Sicco, 9, 14, 23, 57, 160, 161, 162, 163
Mansholt Plan, The ('Agriculture 1980'), 17, 97, 142–3, 165, 167
Marseilles, 145
Marsh, John, 170, 171
Marshall Aid Plan, a, 80
Marshall, Plan, The, 49
Marx, Karl, 37, 86
Mason, Roy, 131
matches, production, 114
Maudling, Reginald, 54
Mauritius, 78
Mayne, Richard, 151, 170
medical profession, the, 88, 89
Medium Term Economic Policy Programmes (MTEPP), 179
mergers, European, of companies, 130, 149, 150
Mexico, 160
Milan, 102
Milk Marketing Board, 170
milk production, 169
Mitbestimmung, 103, 105
Mitchell, Professor John, 31
Mitterand, François, 194
Monaco, 156
monetary problems between Europe and USA, 48
   reserve, common, 139
   union, 11, 27, 124, 137–140
Monnet, Jean, 9
monopolies, 114, 119, 127, 131, 149–51
Monopolies Commission, European, 149
motor industry, 134

multilateral aid, 82
multinational companies, organizations, enterprises, 30, 36, 48–9, 64, 102, 127, 128, 129–32, 139, 186, 198
multi role combat aircraft, 69, 71
mutton, 169

Nabarro, Sir Gerald, 38
NAFTA, 184, 185,
Nairn, Tom, 13, 186
Naples, kingdom of, 144
nation state, the, 5, 7, 13, 17, 20, 84, 85, 131
nationalism 2
National Coal Board, The, 150
nationalization, 117, 118, 119
   of development land, 164
   of multinational companies, 131
NATO (North Atlantic Treaty Organisation), 12, 29, 30, 51, 68, 69, 72, 73
   unofficial assembly of, 34
   strength of forces of, 71
   navy, 71
Nenni, Pietro, 33
Netherlands, The, 14, 32, 36, 80, 85, 110, 111
New Left Review, The, 13
New Statesman, The, 14
New York, stock market, 107
New Zealand, 174
Nietzsche, 93
Nixon, President, 62, 184
Northern Ireland, 39, 62, 112
Norway, 51, 143
Nuclear deterrent, weapons, European, 66, 67, 69, 70, 71, 72, 73, 74, 75
   reactors, 114

OEEC, 12
Official Secrets Acts, 43
Officials, status of Community, 32
oil, 53
oil-producing countries, 81
Ostpolitik, 23, 67, 76

Palestinian refugees, 80
Palliser, Michael, 7
paper industry, 113
Paris, 25, 44, 45
Parliament, the European, 9, 16, 18,
    19, 21, 22, 24, 28–41, 145
  British membership of, 29, 34, 35
  budgetary committee of, 22
  Chamber of Regions, 20, 145
  chambers, numbers of, 29, 36
  direct elections to, 31, 32, 33, 38,
    41, 145, 194
  duration of, 31
  members, 28, 33, 36
  methods of election, 31, 33, 34,
    35, 38, 39
  parties, collaboration between, 36,
    37
  growth of European, 37
  powers of, 28, 29, 31, 32, 34
  revolving, idea for a, 44
  seats, numbers of, 31, 34, 36
  siting of, 44–5
Parker, Charles, 102
'participation', 103
parties, collaboration between see
    European Parliament
  growth of, 37
  transnational, 40
Partido Socialista del Interior (PSI),
    55
Partido Socialista de Obreros Es-
    pañoles (PSOE), 55
Pearson Report, UN, 80
Permanent Representatives, Com-
    mittee of, 16, 20, 21
Perroux, F., 142fn
Pesmazoglou, Professor, 23
Petro-chemical industry, 127, 134
Philipponeau, Michel, 145, 163
Philips of Holland, 150
pig farming, 169
Pinder, John, 145
pipelines, transcontinental com-
    pressed air, 154
Pirelli Company, 102, 130, 150
planification, 178
plant hire, 109, 110

Poland, 64, 163
police, the, 88
political integration, 18, 195
'political secretariat', 17, 25, 45
political union, 155, 193, 194
pollution, 36, 129, 159, 161, 183
Pompidou, President, 7, 10, 18, 25,
    33, 45, 59
population growth, 159, 160, 162
Portugal, 51, 54, 69
Postgate, Raymond, 174
potatoes, 169
Poujade, Robert, 161
poultry farming, 169
Powel, Enoch, 36, 40, 187, 193, 197
power station, nuclear, 135
prices, 168
profit motive, 177
profit-sharing scheme, 103
profit-taxation, 156
profits, transfer of, 130
proportional representation, 39, 40
Proudhon, 8
purchase tax, 156, 158

radar, 133
rail freight, 154
reafforestation, 171
redundancy laws, 100
redundant workers, 144
refrigerator industry, 113, 150
Regions, Chamber of, see Parlia-
    ment, European
regional problems and policies, 9,
    20, 27, 34, 44, 64, 101, 129, 131,
    139, 140, 141–48, 152, 160, 198
Regional Employment Premium,
    141
'Regionale Aktionsprogramme', 142
Remington Rand, 130
Renault, 106
Resistance movements, European, 8
Restrictive Practises Act of 1956,
    125
Rhine coal and iron fields, 9
Rhineland-Palatinate, 147
Rhodesia, 58
Richard, Ivor, 53, 71, 118

Ritson, Christopher, 170, 171
roads, road haulage *see* transport
Roman law, 88
Roman Republic, political system of, 42, 43
Rome, Treaty of, 11, 12, 20, 21, 27, 30, 33, 46, 52, 56, 91, 98, 101, 119, 124, 141, 153, 156, 166 194
Ruhr, 143, 145, 152, 160
Ruhrkohle AG, 150
Rumania, 61, 67
Rumor, Mariano, 65

Saint Gobain glass trust, 102
Saragat, President, 33
Sasse, Christopher, 40, 164, 197
scale, economies of, 130, 131, 135
Science Foundation, the European, 151
Scandinavia, 69
Scarascia Mugnozza, Carlo, 168
Schaus memorandum, 153
Schumann, Robert, 8
    Plan, 10
Scotland, 145, 171
Seton Watson, Hugh, 28
Sicily, 144, 145
ship manufacturing firms, British, 106
shoe manufacturing firms, British, 106
Shonfield, Andrew, 31
Shore, Peter, 1, 172, 181, 187
Short and Medium Term Economic Policy, Committees of, 26–27
Silverman, Sidney, 38
Smith, Arnold, 79
social security, 88, 89, 96, 99, 100
social services, 88, 89, 97, 98, 193
Social Fund, the European, 32, 143
Sovereignty, 12–14
Spain, 51, 55, 56, 57, 85, 153, 174, 189
Special Drawing Rights, 140
Spinelli, Altiero, 6, 8, 13, 15
Statistical Office, European Community (ESCO), 94, 95, 99
Steel, David, 33, 38

Steel Corporation, British, 112, 113
steel industry, 130
sterling, 137, 140
Stewart, Michael, 29, 33, 34, 145
Strachey, John, 87
Strasbourg, 25, 33, 44
students, 90
sugar, 79, 169, 171
supranationalism, 11, 23, 117, 194, 196
Swann, Donald, 46, 168
Sweden, 51, 54, 55, 157, 161, 183
Switzerland, 10, 42, 51, 54, 55, 156
Sykes, Frank, 168, 170

tachograph, 46, 110
tanks, 71
Tanzania, 78
Tariffs, 52, 116, 125, 179
Tatu, Michel, 62
Taxation, 32, 118, 130, 155–8, 161. *See also* VAT
taxis, single unit, 154
Technology, 9, 128, 133–36, 141, 151, 182
technical achievements, British, 106
technocracy, 120
Tenneco, 135
Third World, underdeveloped world, 77–83, 86, 160, 161, 172, 198
Thomassen and Drijner-Verblifa, 150
Times, The, 44
tobacco, 114
tourism, 101
trade preference agreements, 48
Trade Union Congress, 93, 137
    Conference, 157
trade unions, 93, 105, 193
    conference of European, 103
    international, 103, 127, 131
transport, 110, 111, 147, 152–54, 163, 183
Transport Committee, 27
Transport Ministers, European Conference of, 153
Treasury, the, 138

Trotsky, L., 8, 51, 56, 69

VAT (Value Added Tax), 156, 157, 158, 161, 170
Vedel Report, the, 31, 32, 33
Vedel, Georges, 31, 32, 33
Venezuela, 82
Venture, 85
Versailles, Treaty of, 184

Uganda, 78
UN (United Nations), 12, 23, 84
  Economic Commission for Europe, 146
UNCTAD Conference, 23, 80, 82, 83
underdeveloped world *see* Third World
UNEF, 115
unemployment, 95–98, 101, 154
unit trusts, 108
universities, 90
University, European, 89
uranium, 48
urban planning,, 152, 160
Uri, Pierre, 170
USA, 12, 13, 72, 73, 74, 75, 79, 84, 85, 132, 133, 134, 135, 140, 146, 157, 161, 162, 167, 173, 184, 185, 187
  car markets, 113
  economic association with Europe, 49
  foreign policies, 48
  imperialism, 134
  military ally, 47–8, 62
  monetary problems, 48, 53
  multinational companies, 130
  relations with Europe, 47–50
  space industry, 135–6
  special relationship, 49
  stake in industries of Europe, 47, 48, 134
  tariffs, 52
  technological superiority, 48

  trade war with Europe, 132
USSR, 13, 58, 61, 62, 64, 67, 71, 72, 73, 74, 75, 81, 85, 134, 135, 161, 165, 177, 180, 183, 185, 187

Vietnam, 48
Volkswagen, Company, 130

wages, 94, 95, 99, 101, 102
Wales, 144, 145
Wallonia, 142, 145
Warsaw Pact, the, 71, 73
waterways, inland, 110
Weakley, A., 103
weather control, 136
Werner Report plan, 27, 124, 137, 138
West Indies, 79
Westinghouse, 135
WEU (Western European Union), 29, 34, 36
wheat, 169
Wigg, Lord, 75, 195
Williamson, John, 121, 127
Wilson, Harold, 6, 7, 12, 14, 59, 66, 67, 124, 133, 134, 137, 138, 141, 183, 185, 190, 191, 195
Wistrich Ernest, 60
women, position of, 9 12
  workers, 193
Wonnacott, P., 128
Wonnacott, R. J., 128
workers, 26, 94, 100, 193
working hours, 96, 100, 101
Works Constitution Statute, 104
works council, 104
World Parliamentary Association, 84
world reserve unit, 140

Yaoundé Convention, 79, 80
Yugoslavia, 61, 177, 180

Zelletin, Gerda, 37, 38fn
Zollverein, 116, 187